GUIDE TO
CREATION
BASICS

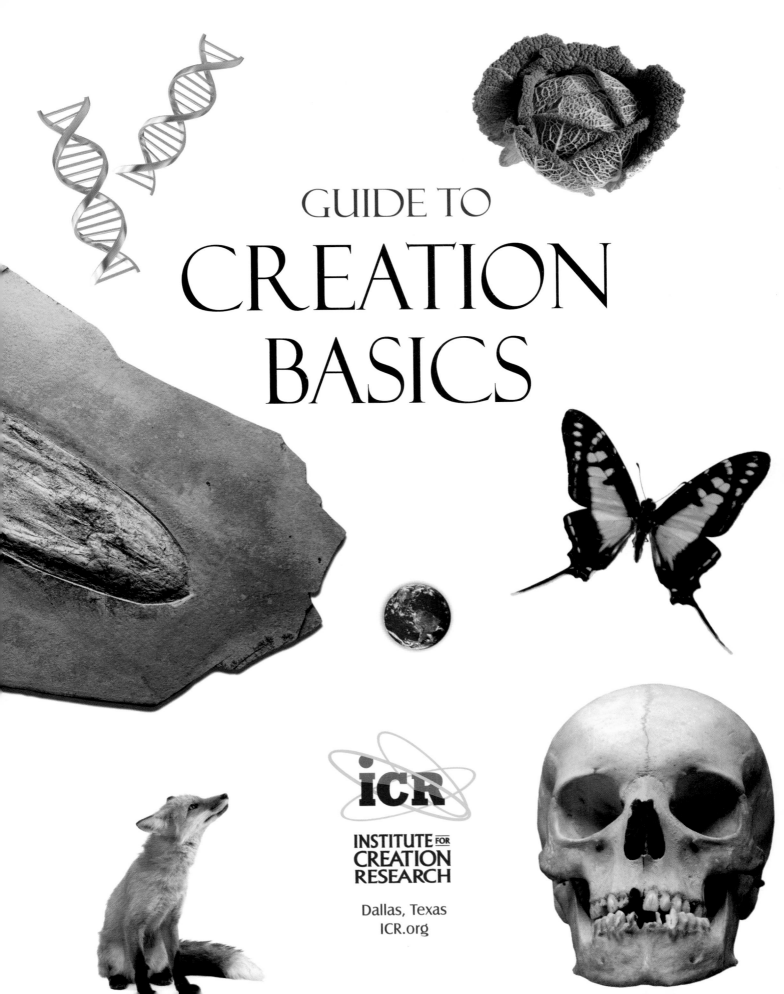

GUIDE TO
CREATION
BASICS

INSTITUTE FOR CREATION RESEARCH

Dallas, Texas
ICR.org

GUIDE TO CREATION BASICS

First printing: May 2013
Sixth printing: October 2021

Unless otherwise noted, all Scripture quotations are from the New King James Version.

ISBN: 978-1-935587-15-6
Library of Congress Catalog Number: 2013938424

Please visit our website for other books and resources: ICR.org

Printed in the United States of America.

Contents

Introduction to Creation

The Earth Sciences

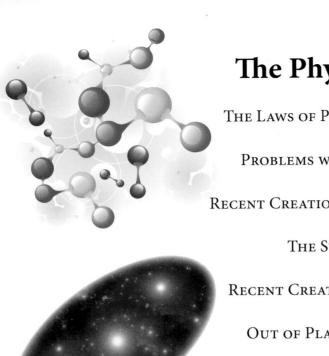

The Physical Sciences

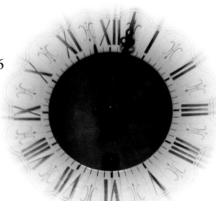

The Life Sciences

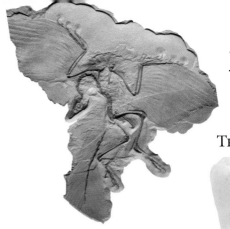

Myths and Fallacies

Foundation to Creation

INTRODUCTION
TO
CREATION

"In the beginning God created the heavens and the earth."
(Genesis 1:1)

Why Study Creation?

Knowing where we came from is extremely important. If mankind is just the end result of mindless natural processes operating over billions of purposeless years, then our lives mean nothing and everything we do is ultimately pointless.

But if God made mankind in His own image to serve a purpose, then each of our lives is packed with meaning. Our Creator specifically set each of us on Earth to play our part according to His excellent and loving plan.

And if the biblical account of creation is true—if God really created the world in six literal days, just as Genesis says—then we can be sure that the rest of the Bible's message is true. We can be confident that it is worthy of our complete trust in all matters, whether of science, faith, or the way we should live our lives.

Why should we study God's creation? In short, it's because that investigation will help answer our most significant questions about life, the world, its origin, its purpose—and ultimately why we are here.

What can God's creation tell me about its Creator?

A Framework of History

Facts don't always speak for themselves, and each person interprets what they see according to what they believe. Our beliefs about the past become the keys to understanding history. Imagine trying to reconstruct the detailed series of events that occurred on a Civil War battlefield. You might find some bullets, but they don't tell much. The way to learn history is to study what those near to the experience said about it, and then see how the evidence supports that account. Similarly, we learn more about the history of the world by studying what the first people recorded, not by just examining fossils, DNA, or planets. Scripture includes accounts by those who, while recording their experiences with God, recorded history.

With no written records, one could interpret scattered Civil War bullets in any number of ways. But those artifacts hold great significance when interpreted according to reliable history. In the same way, the evidence of creation holds great significance in the context of scriptural history. And all the information—whether from outer space, animal life, or inside the earth—matches what the Bible says.

If the things scientists write oppose what the Bible says, whom do I believe and why?

Biblical History	Secular History
Earth is thousands of years old.	Earth is billions of years old.
Life comes from the living God.	Life comes from non-living matter and energy.
Creatures are well-designed by a supernatural Creator.	Creatures are cobbled together by natural processes.
Members of the same kind are related.	All creatures are related.
Death occurs after sin entered the world.	Death occurs before sin entered the world.

Why is the world so perfectly fit for life but at the same time full of imperfections?

The Wonder of It All

One more significant reason to study God's creation is simple and often overlooked—to appreciate God for what He has done. From the intricate design of DNA molecules to the grand display of stars, any person who knows and trusts the great Creator has the privilege of giving praise, not to the creation itself, but to the One who made it all!

Finding Answers

It is human nature to want to understand our world better and to better understand our place in it. Scientific inquiry allows us to gain a deeper knowledge of the universe, life on Earth, and the Creator of all things. While we can't know everything, we can understand some basics.

The Limits of Science

Most questions about origins are out of reach of lab-based science. We cannot perform a test-tube experiment to measure the character of God, nor can we test whether or not humans were created, since that is a one-time event that occurred in the past. But there are other ways to learn about purposes and origins. Scientific discoveries can improve our lives and put a man on the moon, but science cannot answer every question.

Influenced by Our Beliefs

People tend to approach the question of origins with ideas already in place about how everything got started. This is good if we have the right understanding because it saves time trying to repeatedly verify the truthfulness of each word or observation we encounter. But this is bad if we have some wrong ideas. What we see in the earth, seas, and skies does not provide our ideas about where we came from. Instead, we fit the evidence into what we already believe.

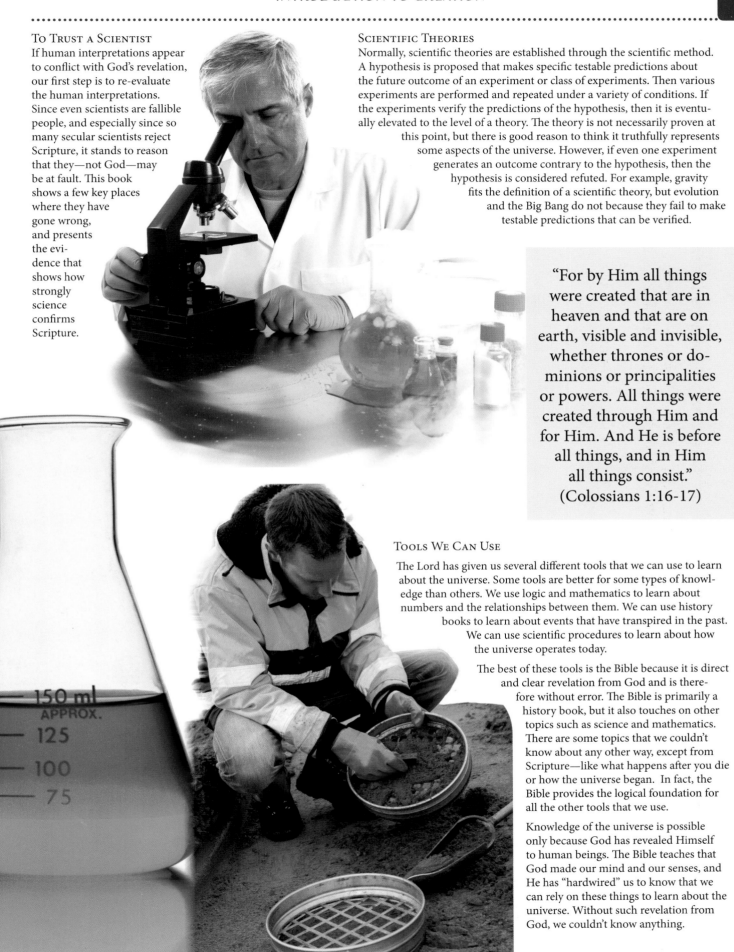

To Trust a Scientist

If human interpretations appear to conflict with God's revelation, our first step is to re-evaluate the human interpretations. Since even scientists are fallible people, and especially since so many secular scientists reject Scripture, it stands to reason that they—not God—may be at fault. This book shows a few key places where they have gone wrong, and presents the evidence that shows how strongly science confirms Scripture.

Scientific Theories

Normally, scientific theories are established through the scientific method. A hypothesis is proposed that makes specific testable predictions about the future outcome of an experiment or class of experiments. Then various experiments are performed and repeated under a variety of conditions. If the experiments verify the predictions of the hypothesis, then it is eventually elevated to the level of a theory. The theory is not necessarily proven at this point, but there is good reason to think it truthfully represents some aspects of the universe. However, if even one experiment generates an outcome contrary to the hypothesis, then the hypothesis is considered refuted. For example, gravity fits the definition of a scientific theory, but evolution and the Big Bang do not because they fail to make testable predictions that can be verified.

> "For by Him all things were created that are in heaven and that are on earth, visible and invisible, whether thrones or dominions or principalities or powers. All things were created through Him and for Him. And He is before all things, and in Him all things consist."
> (Colossians 1:16-17)

Tools We Can Use

The Lord has given us several different tools that we can use to learn about the universe. Some tools are better for some types of knowledge than others. We use logic and mathematics to learn about numbers and the relationships between them. We can use history books to learn about events that have transpired in the past. We can use scientific procedures to learn about how the universe operates today.

The best of these tools is the Bible because it is direct and clear revelation from God and is therefore without error. The Bible is primarily a history book, but it also touches on other topics such as science and mathematics. There are some topics that we couldn't know about any other way, except from Scripture—like what happens after you die or how the universe began. In fact, the Bible provides the logical foundation for all the other tools that we use.

Knowledge of the universe is possible only because God has revealed Himself to human beings. The Bible teaches that God made our mind and our senses, and He has "hardwired" us to know that we can rely on these things to learn about the universe. Without such revelation from God, we couldn't know anything.

In the Beginning

"In the beginning, God created the heavens and the earth" (Genesis 1:1). The Bible tells us who God is—the triune Creator God who chose to make mankind in His image and who reveals Himself through Christ Jesus and the Bible. Specifically, the first book of the Bible, Genesis, reveals what we could never know otherwise about origins, such as where we came from, how we got here, and why God made us. No other source does that.

According to the Bible, God created all things. Scientists study nature in order to better understand the world around us, and while the Bible doesn't give us all the scientific data, it does provide the basic framework within which we can interpret scientific observations. Evaluating evidence is a key component in the search for truth, not

Six Days of Creation

DAY 1

In the beginning God created the heavens and the earth. The earth was without form, and void; and darkness was on the face of the deep. And the Spirit of God was hovering over the face of the waters. (Genesis 1:1-2)
God established the triune nature of the universe on the first day—the beginning (time), the heavens (space), and the earth (matter). He also established the definition for a day: "God divided the light from the darkness. God called the light Day, and the darkness He called Night. So the evening and the morning were the first day" (Genesis 1:4-5).

DAY 2

Then God said, "Let there be a firmament in the midst of the waters, and let it divide the waters from the waters." Thus God made the firmament, and divided the waters which were under the firmament from the waters which were above the firmament; and it was so. And God called the firmament Heaven. So the evening and the morning were the second day. (Genesis 1:6-8)
God shaped the "firmament," or the atmosphere. He also divided the surface water ("waters below the firmament") from the "waters above the firmament." Liquid water and the earth's atmosphere are essential and perfectly suited for living things, and God's activities on the second day show that He intended to make Earth a special place.

DAY 3

Then God said, "Let the waters under the heavens be gathered together into one place, and let the dry land appear"; and it was so. And God called the dry land Earth, and the gathering together of the waters He called Seas. And God saw that it was good. Then God said, "Let the earth bring forth grass, the herb that yields seed, and the fruit tree that yields fruit according to its kind, whose seed is in itself, on the earth"; and it was so. And the earth brought forth grass, the herb that yields seed according to its kind, and the tree that yields fruit, whose seed is in itself according to its kind. And God saw that it was good. So the evening and the morning were the third day. (Genesis 1:9-13)
Under God's commands, Earth began taking shape. He set boundaries for the waters and made the dry land appear, which allowed for grass, herbs (shrubs and bushes), and trees. The grass, herbs, and trees were the first part of creation that God gave the ability to reproduce "after its kind."

only in science but also in other areas of life.

Genesis details God's acts during the six 24-hour days of the creation week. It also describes how He made and shaped what He created into an organized and functioning cosmos that He declared to be "very good" at the end of the first chapter.

Bees were not around yet to pollinate flowers on Day Three, so plants would not have been able to reproduce if very much time separated the creation of the plants and the creation of animals.

DAY 4

Then God said, "Let there be lights in the firmament of the heavens to divide the day from the night; and let them be for signs and seasons, and for days and years; and let them be for lights in the firmament of the heavens to give light on the earth"; and it was so. Then God made two great lights: the greater light to rule the day, and the lesser light to rule the night. He made the stars also. God set them in the firmament of the heavens to give light on the earth, and to rule over the day and over the night, and to divide the light from the darkness. And God saw that it was good. So the evening and the morning were the fourth day. (Genesis 1:14-19)

On the fourth day of the creation week, God made the sun, moon, and the stars. He said these would be for keeping track of the passing of time ("signs and seasons, and for days and years"). As almost an afterthought, "He made the stars also."

DAY 5

Then God said, "Let the waters abound with an abundance of living creatures, and let birds fly above the earth across the face of the firmament of the heavens." So God created great sea creatures and every living thing that moves, with which the waters abounded, according to their kind, and every winged bird according to its kind. And God saw that it was good. And God blessed them, saying, "Be fruitful and multiply, and fill the waters in the seas, and let birds multiply on the earth." So the evening and the morning were the fifth day. (Genesis 1:20-23)

On the fifth day, God made the animals that would live in the water and fly in the air. After plants, this is the second time He made living things that could reproduce. But unlike plants, these creatures could move about on their own.

DAY 6

Then God said, "Let the earth bring forth the living creature according to its kind: cattle and creeping thing and beast of the earth, each according to its kind"; and it was so. . . . Then God said, "Let Us make man in Our image, according to Our likeness; let them have dominion over the fish of the sea, over the birds of the air, and over the cattle, over all the earth and over every creeping thing that creeps on the earth." So God created man in His own image; in the image of God He created him; male and female He created them. . . . Then God saw everything that He had made, and indeed it was very good. So the evening and the morning were the sixth day. (Genesis 1:24-31)

On the sixth day, God created all the land animals and humans. The Bible describes how God created people separate from the animals, making man and woman "in His own image." He also gave people the responsibility to "rule" or take care of the rest of the creation.

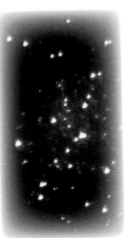

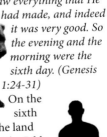

THE EARTH
SCIENCES

*"And God called the dry land
Earth, and the gathering
together of the waters
He called Seas."
(Genesis 1:10)*

The great Flood of Noah's day was a cata-strophic event unlike anything mankind has witnessed in recent ages. It is also the best way to explain the major geologic features on Earth's surface.

Genesis 7 states that during the Flood "all the fountains of the great deep were broken up, and the windows of heaven were opened. And the rain was on the earth forty days and forty nights. . . . And the waters prevailed exceedingly on the earth, and all the high hills under the whole heaven were covered. . . . And the waters prevailed on the earth one hundred and fifty days" (Genesis 7:11-12, 19, 24).

The Flood Explains Rock Layers

Most of the rock strata that we see today are sedimentary layers, which formed when large amounts of fast-moving dirty water deposited sediment. The water then drained away in a relatively short time (from hours to a few years), leaving the sediment to dry and harden into rock. Some of the best examples of fast-forming sedimentary rock strata are the ones that formed after Mount St. Helens erupted in 1980. Within just a few years, explosive muddy eruptions filled the nearby valley with sediment layers up to 600 feet thick. And in one afternoon in 1982, a "tsunami" of water from the melted glacier on top of the volcano carved a canyon, allowing us to see those layers.

Scripture tells us that it not only rained, but that *all* of the "fountains of the great deep were broken up." This could refer to volcanic activity, which suggests movement in Earth's crustal plates. Immense energy over a short time was needed to move the plates, and the Flood that the Bible describes best explains the earth we see today.

The Flood Explains Mountains and Valleys

Earth's surface is not flat. It has some flat areas, but it also has irregularities such as mountains and valleys. Many mountains formed when Earth's crustal plates collided and caused the land masses to rise. Valleys with steep-sided walls formed when huge amounts of water quickly drained away ("the waters decreased"—Genesis 8:3). Both mountain-uplifting and valley-carving required immense amounts of energy, which is what came from the great Flood. Rapid mountain-uplift from the Flood also explains why fossils of marine creatures that once lived on the ocean floor can be found on the highest mountain peaks.

Mt. Everest

THE FLOOD EXPLAINS FOSSILS

Almost all fossils are found within sedimentary rocks that are packed with clues that tell of their deposition by fast-moving water. For example, the overwhelming majority of fossils are of marine creatures like clams, coral, trilobites, and fish. A smaller number of fossils are of land creatures, including dinosaurs, lizards, birds, and small mammals. (Layers containing dinosaur fossils very often contain clams, fish, and mammals, too.) An enormous but short-lived flood was necessary to bury the creatures quickly and completely to prevent scavenging and then to compress the sediment enough for the remains to fossilize rather than to rot.

THE FLOOD EXPLAINS TECTONICS

How can you move an entire continent? There simply is no way to do it using the forces we see now. The required spreading speed would have been much greater in the past and the forces more dynamic and quite different from those acting today. In general, a planet-wide cataclysm like the great Flood of Noah's day, which restructured the globe, must have been involved, and the conditions must have been very different from what we observe today. The Flood cataclysm morphed the early earth into the earth we know now.

Most fossils are of marine creatures, and they had to be buried rapidly by a great deal of water and sediment in order to turn into fossils. The best way to explain their existence is the Flood of Noah's day.

This marine fossil was found on Mt. Everest, the tallest mountain in the world. The best way to explain how an ocean creature got to the top of a mountain is that the great Flood formed many sedimentary layers on the ocean floor that hardened and later buckled up into mountains.

Laboratory tests have shown that coal can form in a matter of days or hours. After Mount St. Helens erupted in 1980, researchers found a charred log with one end that had turned into coal almost instantly. Large coal deposits found all over the world show that a global catastrophe like the Flood was needed to make them.

In addition to being the best explanation for mountains and valleys, the great Flood also makes the most sense of coal deposits, petrified forests, and a host of other features on Earth.

The Flood According to the Bible

Where did all the Flood's water come from? How did all the animals get on board Noah's Ark? What about the dinosaurs? The Bible and sound science provide the answers.

Scripture says that the great Flood of Noah's day covered the mountains, implying a deep flood. But it also covered "all the high hills that were under the whole heaven" (Genesis 7:19-20). The "whole heaven" means the entire atmosphere. Since the atmosphere is worldwide, the Flood was worldwide. While the Bible specifies that it began with a special rain for *40 days and nights*, the Flood lasted about *one year*. The water rose for the first five months, prevailed over the land, and then abated or drained away.

Scripture does not give us all the details of the Flood events, but geology fills in the blanks. God's primary purpose for the great Flood was to totally annihilate the continents and the life they held. The Flood involved much more than water flooding the land, standing above the mountains for a while, and then draining. Moving water contains much energy, while standing water does little work. God promised He was going to destroy the wicked and violent inhabitants of Earth along with the earth itself. The super-powered cleansing floodwaters—washing "back and forth" across the land—appear to be the tool God chose to accomplish that cleansing of Earth (Genesis 8:3).

WHERE DID THE WATER COME FROM?

The oceans cover about 70 percent of the globe, and the oceans on average are much deeper than the continents are high. If Earth's surface were completely level, with no deep oceans and no high continents, the oceans would cover the entire globe to a depth of about a mile and a half. There was plenty of water available for the Flood, and it came when "all the fountains of the great deep were broken up, and the windows of heaven were opened" (Genesis 7:11).

A satellite image of the Pacific Ocean. Earth's surface is mostly covered in water, and the ocean basins are deeper than the mountains on the continents are high. The water from the Flood is still here.

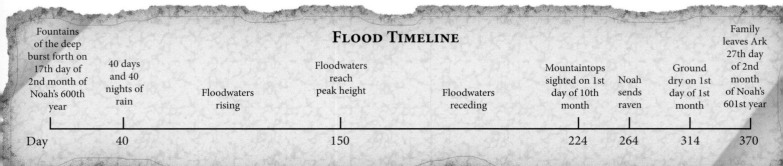

FLOOD TIMELINE

Fountains of the deep burst forth on 17th day of 2nd month of Noah's 600th year	40 days and 40 nights of rain	Floodwaters rising	Floodwaters reach peak height	Floodwaters receding	Mountaintops sighted on 1st day of 10th month	Noah sends raven	Ground dry on 1st day of 1st month	Family leaves Ark 27th day of 2nd month of Noah's 601st year
Day	40		150		224	264	314	370

Volume: ~1.5 million cubic feet
Gross tonnage: ~13,960 tons
Freight capacity: ~500 railroad stock cars
Able to carry about 125,000 sheep-size animals

~450 feet

~75 feet

~45 feet

THE ANIMALS ON THE ARK

Scripture tells us the size of the Ark was about 450 feet long, 75 feet wide, and 45 feet high—about 1.5 million cubic feet of space. The animal kinds were commanded to come in pairs. Nearly all animals have an instinctive ability to migrate when faced with danger and enter a hibernation-like state until the danger passes. Maybe God, the Creator of animals, instilled these abilities into each chosen pair, and all of their descendants retain them.

An animal "kind" probably relates to the potential to interbreed. For instance, domestic dogs can mate with coyotes and wolves, and thus they would be within the same kind even though they are categorized as different species today. Only two representatives of the dog kind or the cat kind were on the Ark. Post-Flood adaptations have produced our modern animal varieties.

Generous estimates place the total number of animals on the Ark at fewer than 25,000 pairs. The average size of all animals is surprisingly small. There are only a few large animals, but many small ones, with the average size being smaller than a medium-size dog. All these animals and the food they needed easily fit on board the Ark.

DINOSAURS ON THE ARK

Since God made dinosaurs during the creation week, and since we have abundant evidence showing that humans and dinosaurs lived at the same time in the same places, then that means dinosaurs were on the Ark. They were a special category of reptiles, so we can look at other large reptiles to see how they were able to fit on board. Many of the larger reptiles like crocodiles and snakes live for many years and do not stop growing throughout their lives. The Ark's purpose was survival of the animal kinds, so God would not have chosen the oldest, largest specimens to go aboard. More likely, He would have selected young, strong ones that were able to reproduce. Crocodiles and snakes are quite small when they are young, so the dinosaurs aboard the Ark were probably also small juveniles.

DID YOU KNOW?

God instructed Noah to take on the Ark *seven* of each of the clean animals and of the birds of the sky (Genesis 7:2-3).

The purpose of the Ark was to preserve two of each kind of animal that would later be able to reproduce and repopulate Earth. The animals God selected to be saved would have been young and healthy to accomplish this purpose. So, most of the animals on the Ark were not large—even the dinosaurs.

The two peaks Lesser Ararat and Greater Ararat in modern-day Turkey. Genesis 8:4 says that after the floodwaters decreased, the Ark landed "on the mountains of Ararat."

Flood Deposits Are Often Continent-Wide

Noah evidently had 120 years of warning that the Flood was coming (Genesis 6:3). In this amount of time, he, his family, and the animals could have walked around the world several times. There was no need for the Ark if the Flood was only local. And if the great Flood was local, it failed its main mission of destroying all humans and land animals, and God lied to us when He said He would never send another flood like it (Genesis 9:15), for there have been many local floods. But God does not lie.

Geologic evidence for the Flood reveals its catastrophic origin and widespread nature. The Flood, while global, was not necessarily acting the same at all points on the globe at every moment.

SEDIMENTARY DEPOSITS

The majority of sedimentary deposits are extremely fine-grained, like shale, originally deposited as mud. But the tiny grains of mud only collect today on the ocean bottom in still water. The grains filter down through the water at a very slow rate, sometimes taking months to reach the bottom. No long-term calm-water location can be found in today's world because there are always currents and water disturbances that keep the grains suspended. Yet the world abounds with such "mud rocks." Something caused the grains to adhere to one another in a clump. This happens in laboratory experiments only when the water is treated with unusual chemicals. But as larger agglomerations, they fall easily through the water and can flow down a gradual slope. Such a fortuitous combination of circumstances can hardly happen in nature today and could never occur on a wide scale. But during the Flood, they would happen and could account for the vast deposits of shale and other mudrocks all around us.

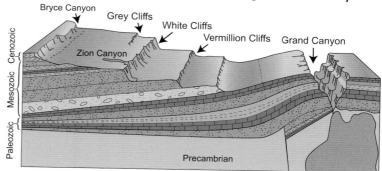

Grand Canyon possesses deposits left during the early Flood, while Zion Canyon has layers from the middle Flood, and Bryce Canyon shows those from the late (and post) Flood. The individual layers, not all of which are pictured here, are typically vast and of catastrophic origin—the signature of the great Flood of Noah's day.

THE GREAT UNCONFORMITY

Right below the horizontal layers is an erosion surface so extensive that it is called the Great Unconformity. It seems the first burst of the Flood accomplished unthinkable erosion and then began to deposit large sand grains and then smaller sand grains. This sandstone can be traced throughout Grand Canyon and north into Utah. A nearly identical layer rests in Europe and across the northern hemisphere. Secular geologists have traditionally taught that the Great Unconformity was deposited by normal waves as a shoreline migrated across the continent, but there is evidence that the depositional agent must have been a series of massive underwater flows of sandy mud that would have been present in a worldwide flood.

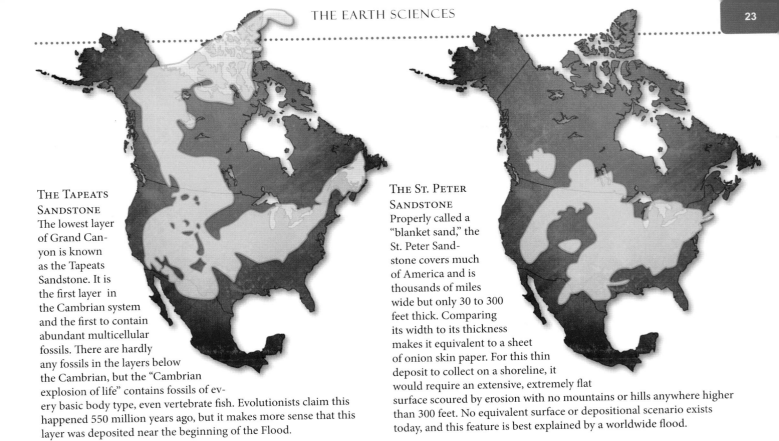

THE TAPEATS SANDSTONE

The lowest layer of Grand Canyon is known as the Tapeats Sandstone. It is the first layer in the Cambrian system and the first to contain abundant multicellular fossils. There are hardly any fossils in the layers below the Cambrian, but the "Cambrian explosion of life" contains fossils of every basic body type, even vertebrate fish. Evolutionists claim this happened 550 million years ago, but it makes more sense that this layer was deposited near the beginning of the Flood.

THE ST. PETER SANDSTONE

Properly called a "blanket sand," the St. Peter Sandstone covers much of America and is thousands of miles wide but only 30 to 300 feet thick. Comparing its width to its thickness makes it equivalent to a sheet of onion skin paper. For this thin deposit to collect on a shoreline, it would require an extensive, extremely flat surface scoured by erosion with no mountains or hills anywhere higher than 300 feet. No equivalent surface or depositional scenario exists today, and this feature is best explained by a worldwide flood.

MEGASEQUENCES

Each grouping of sedimentary layers (called a megasequence) contains features best understood as a transgression of the ocean onto the continents, followed by a regression of the waters back into the sea and the resulting erosion, followed by a second sequence, and then another. Uniformitarians interpret each sequence as having taken many millions of years.

Genesis 8:3 (KJV) says, "And the waters returned from off the earth continually: and after the end of the hundred and fifty days the waters were abated." Although the King James Version uses the word "continually," the Hebrew phrase connotes the water motion as being continually "to and fro" or "back and forth"—the waters were continually going and returning. A repetitive back-and-forth movement of floodwaters is the evidence we observe as megasequences in the geologic record of the Flood. The sedimentary rocks and fossils left in the floodwaters' wake contain abundant evidence of the waters transgressing over the continents and then regressing back into the ocean.

The Coconino Sandstone is a 300- to 400-foot-thick layer of white sandstone near the top of the Grand Canyon. Secular geologists maintain that this layer was laid down by wind currents like sand dunes are in the deserts today. But cross-bedding and other features in the sandstone show that it was actually laid down by water near the mid-point of the Genesis Flood.

Bryce Canyon, Utah (left)
Grand Canyon, Arizona (below)

The Flood Was Catastrophic

The great Flood of Noah's day was catastrophic and global in nature. Some have argued that it was a local flood that Noah witnessed, but this is not what Scripture says. Genesis 7:19-24 states:

> And the waters prevailed exceedingly on the earth, and all the high hills under the whole heaven were covered. The waters prevailed fifteen cubits upward, and the mountains were covered. . . . So He destroyed all living things which were on the face of the ground: both man and cattle, creeping thing and bird of the air. They were destroyed from the earth. Only Noah and those who were with him in the ark remained alive. And the waters prevailed on the earth one hundred and fifty days.

It was a horrific time during which God rightfully exercised justice upon sinful mankind. Humans had disobeyed Him repeatedly, and they received the destruction they deserved. Only Noah, who had "found grace in the eyes of the LORD" (Genesis 6:8), survived with his immediate family and a pair of each land-dwelling animal kind aboard the Ark that God had instructed him to build.

Evidence all around the world shows that the entire earth was once flooded. In fact, it is safe to hypothesize that the world looks completely different now than it did before the Flood.

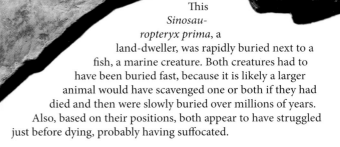

This *Sinosauropteryx prima*, a land-dweller, was rapidly buried next to a fish, a marine creature. Both creatures had to have been buried fast, because it is likely a larger animal would have scavenged one or both if they had died and then were slowly buried over millions of years. Also, based on their positions, both appear to have struggled just before dying, probably having suffocated.

ANIMALS FROM MIXED HABITATS

Fossil graveyards often contain numerous animals from differing habitats. Saltwater fish are sometimes found with upland dwellers. Crocodile fossils are found with deep sea denizens and desert and arctic mammals. They could scarcely be lumped together in this way by the uniform processes of today. Some great cataclysm is needed to explain what we see, and more secular scientists are adopting the notion that fossils formed in environments with large amounts of fast-moving water and sediments.

Unlike other reptiles that lay eggs, this ichthyosaur apparently gave birth to live young. This fossil shows that it must have been buried extremely quickly, since the entire process of giving birth would not have taken much time. This fossil shows that the creature and her young died and were rapidly buried as sediments and water cascaded upon them, not through a slow accumulation of sediments around a dead animal.

INDICATIONS OF VIOLENT DEATH

Secular scientists tend to interpret fossil creatures as having died and been buried over millions of years. However, fossil remains of creatures are often found in death poses. The famous *Archaeopteryx* bird fossil lies with its neck and tail arched back as if it were dying a horrible, drowning death. Clams are found with both halves tightly shut—"clammed up," as living clams do to protect themselves from danger. Dinosaur fossils, also in death poses, are found ripped apart but often not scavenged by other animals. Fossilized creatures give every indication they were violently killed and/or transported by moving water or mud to the places we now find them.

Cross-beds show sedimentary layers that are not parallel. Instead, they cross one another. Cross-bedded angles are consistent with deposition under deep, fast-flowing water, not by wind, as many secular geologists assume. Two of the most well-known cross-bedded sandstones are the Navajo and Coconino Sandstones.

Most fossils are from marine creatures that were buried together rapidly with other marine animals and even land animals. As researchers study these formations more, we learn that these "fossil jumbles" contain creatures that evolutionists thought existed millions of years apart and yet are buried side by side in the same rock layers.

FOSSILS ARE FOUND MOSTLY ON CONTINENTS

The catastrophic deposits in which the (mostly marine) fossils are found are located on almost all continents. A series of marine cataclysms inundated the land, destroying nearly everything there and laying down a record plain enough for all of us to see. Terrestrial (land creature) fossils primarily come from the Ice Age that followed the great Flood.

NO COMPLETE ECOSYSTEMS

Fossils are usually entombed in deposits with no complete ecosystems present that could have supported them in life. Often, evolutionists portray a fossil's tomb as a snapshot of its life and use it to build stories about the creature's habits. But these plants and animals are not necessarily found where they lived or where they died. They are found where they were buried, and it is not good science to presume patterns of life from the transported remains of once-living things.

A fish in the process of eating another fish. If this fossil formed over a long period of time, then it is unlikely that the larger fish would have still been eating the smaller one. Both creatures were buried and died quickly in a catastrophe like the Flood.

Mountains often formed when Earth's crustal plates collided and caused the land masses to thrust upward. Valleys with steep-sided walls formed when enormous amounts of water quickly drained ("the waters were abated"—Genesis 8:3, KJV). Both mountain-uplift and valley-carving required immense amounts of energy such as the great Flood provided.

**Carved by a catastrophe,
Earth's mountains and canyons
point to the power of God.**

Grand Canyon, Arizona, USA

Fossils from the Flood

A fossil is the preserved remains of a once-living thing. It can be an impression left in rock, a hard or soft body part replaced by minerals, or original body parts. What does it take to make these fossils?

Scientists have to form best guesses about fossilization, since we do not generally observe the process today. But the rock layers in which we find most of the world's fossils provide enough clues for us to reconstruct the basics. First, the creature had to be buried quickly in mud or sand. Otherwise, its remains would have been scavenged by other animals or decomposed by microbes, leaving nothing to fossilize. Second, the mud or sand must have been moving with more force and speed than the fossilized creature could exert. Otherwise, it would just leave. Fossils of large and powerful creatures, like 50-foot-long dinosaurs, mosasaurs, or whales, imply *tremendous* forces. Third, fast-flowing water is the best way to explain the mixture of land and sea creatures found in fossil layers, like dinosaurs and mammals with fish and clams. And finally, that same water must have soon drained, leaving the mud, sand, and buried animal remains stranded in high-elevation locations. Otherwise, longstanding water would have allowed chemicals and microbes to quickly dissolve and degrade the remains, leaving nothing to fossilize.

Noah's global Flood provides the power needed to deposit fossils in rock layers all over the world's continents, even on the highest mountains. The Flood's waters took several months to drain away, exposing the layers. Enormous Ice Age storms after the Flood drowned animals and even some humans, producing the Ice Age fossils that are nearest Earth's surface.

Weathering quickly erases fresh footprints. How were these preserved? Apparently, water flowed across large land areas with enough vigor to carry and spread enormous blankets of sediment, covering and protecting the tracks. Each new sediment "blanket" filled in the fresh tracks. Creation geologists suggest that this occurred at the apex of the Flood year, during a pause between waters inundating all the land and then flowing off the newly formed continents.

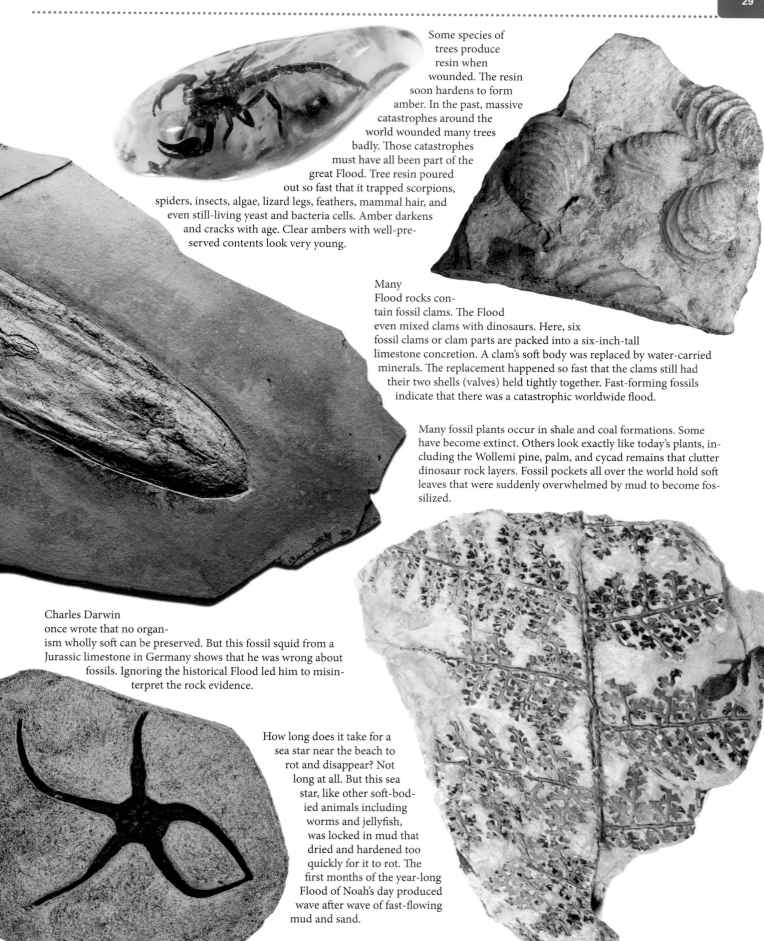

Some species of trees produce resin when wounded. The resin soon hardens to form amber. In the past, massive catastrophes around the world wounded many trees badly. Those catastrophes must have all been part of the great Flood. Tree resin poured out so fast that it trapped scorpions, spiders, insects, algae, lizard legs, feathers, mammal hair, and even still-living yeast and bacteria cells. Amber darkens and cracks with age. Clear ambers with well-preserved contents look very young.

Many Flood rocks contain fossil clams. The Flood even mixed clams with dinosaurs. Here, six fossil clams or clam parts are packed into a six-inch-tall limestone concretion. A clam's soft body was replaced by water-carried minerals. The replacement happened so fast that the clams still had their two shells (valves) held tightly together. Fast-forming fossils indicate that there was a catastrophic worldwide flood.

Many fossil plants occur in shale and coal formations. Some have become extinct. Others look exactly like today's plants, including the Wollemi pine, palm, and cycad remains that clutter dinosaur rock layers. Fossil pockets all over the world hold soft leaves that were suddenly overwhelmed by mud to become fossilized.

Charles Darwin once wrote that no organism wholly soft can be preserved. But this fossil squid from a Jurassic limestone in Germany shows that he was wrong about fossils. Ignoring the historical Flood led him to misinterpret the rock evidence.

How long does it take for a sea star near the beach to rot and disappear? Not long at all. But this sea star, like other soft-bodied animals including worms and jellyfish, was locked in mud that dried and hardened too quickly for it to rot. The first months of the year-long Flood of Noah's day produced wave after wave of fast-flowing mud and sand.

The Fossil Record

The standard geologic column pictured on this page appears to have fossils of long-ago organisms near the bottom, less ancient ones toward the middle, and recent fossils near the top. This supposedly shows the progression of evolution over time from simple to more complex life forms. But the bottom rock layers were actually deposited at the start of the Flood, and the ones near the top were laid down later in the Flood. The bottom layers document the early bursts of the "fountains of the great deep" (Genesis 7:11) and accompanying tsunamis, which would have primarily impacted ocean bottom dwellers. Following episodes would have buried upper marine life and then coastal life. So, the fossil record actually shows the stages of the great Flood.

Fossil fern

Because there is no evidence that any particular animal ever morphed into a fundamentally different type of animal, evolutionists came up with a hypothesis called "punctuated equilibrium" in which evolutionary development is marked by isolated episodes of rapid speciation in between long periods of little change. But the species changes touted by punctuated equilibrium are either common variations of individual offspring or adaptations of a population to differing conditions, *not* large-scale macroevolution.

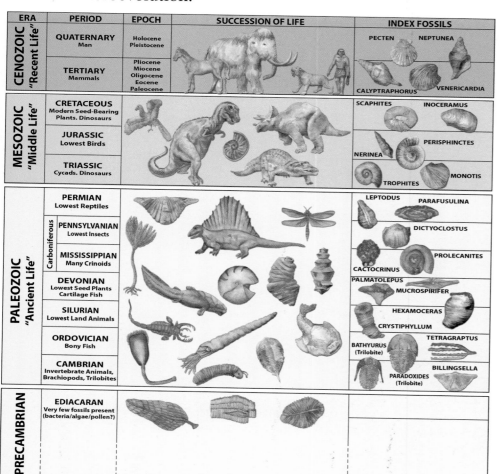

ERA	PERIOD	EPOCH	SUCCESSION OF LIFE	INDEX FOSSILS
CENOZOIC "Recent Life"	QUATERNARY Man	Holocene Pleistocene		PECTEN, NEPTUNEA
CENOZOIC "Recent Life"	TERTIARY Mammals	Pliocene Miocene Oligocene Eocene Paleocene		CALYPTRAPHORUS, VENERICARDIA
MESOZOIC "Middle Life"	CRETACEOUS Modern Seed-Bearing Plants. Dinosaurs			SCAPHITES, INOCERAMUS
MESOZOIC "Middle Life"	JURASSIC Lowest Birds			NERINEA, PERISPHINCTES
MESOZOIC "Middle Life"	TRIASSIC Cycads. Dinosaurs			TROPHITES, MONOTIS
PALEOZOIC "Ancient Life"	PERMIAN Lowest Reptiles			LEPTODUS, PARAFUSULINA
PALEOZOIC "Ancient Life"	Carboniferous PENNSYLVANIAN Lowest Insects			DICTYOCLOSTUS
PALEOZOIC "Ancient Life"	Carboniferous MISSISSIPPIAN Many Crinoids			CACTOCRINUS, PROLECANITES
PALEOZOIC "Ancient Life"	DEVONIAN Lowest Seed Plants Cartilage Fish			PALMATOLEPUS, MUCROSPIRIFER
PALEOZOIC "Ancient Life"	SILURIAN Lowest Land Animals			HEXAMOCERAS, CRYSTIPHYLLUM
PALEOZOIC "Ancient Life"	ORDOVICIAN Bony Fish			BATHYURUS (Trilobite), TETRAGRAPTUS
PALEOZOIC "Ancient Life"	CAMBRIAN Invertebrate Animals, Brachiopods, Trilobites			PARADOXIDES (Trilobite), BILLINGSELLA
PRECAMBRIAN	EDIACARAN Very few fossils present (bacteria/algae/pollen?)			

Macroevolution refers to large change, e.g., particles to people, dinosaur to bird, ape to man, etc.

SUDDEN APPEARANCE OF BASIC TYPES

The fossil record shows a large variety of creatures, but variety is not evolution. Cats and dogs appear to have been suddenly created to live in similar environments, breathe the same air, eat the same foods, and survive with similar blood. But cats have kittens and dogs have puppies. They did not originate by mutations in a different type of common ancestor, nor did one come from the other. This true-to-type consistency is what the fossils show in other animal types as well.

MANY FOSSILS FOUND THROUGHOUT THE GEOLOGIC COLUMN

Various fossil types are found in many layers, with more fossil ranges being continually extended by new discoveries. Statistical treatments give reason to believe that essentially all types lived throughout a large portion of history.

Macroevolution is typically described as a natural process that generates new biological structures from less-ordered material.

COMPLEXITY AT THE START

Each plant or animal alive today exhibits amazing complexity, and each of their body parts is precisely designed to perform its function. All parts work together for the good of the whole, and there often is no use for a particular part without the others. And all essential parts must be present for any to accomplish any useful purpose. Evolution necessitates the gradual accumulation of body parts through random mutation and amalgamation of previous parts with different functions into a new whole. The elegance of design, however, argues *against* a patchwork origin and *for* an intelligent cause.

Trilobite

EXTINCTION, NOT EVOLUTION

Extinction is well-documented in the fossil record. While extinction is a necessary part of the evolutionary scenario, it is not evolution. It is more like the opposite. Speciation within basic kinds is different from the introduction of new kinds, and evolution requires a dizzying array of basic new kinds. The origination of a new form has never been documented in the modern world of scientific observation, but several species go extinct every day. The fossils show this also occurred in the past.

MOST FOSSILS ARE MARINE INVERTEBRATES

At least 95 percent of all animal fossils are of marine invertebrates well-designed for life in the sea. Some lived in high-energy, near-shore environments, but others lived in the deep ocean away from the pounding action of the waves. The majority of vertebrate fossils are fish—again, mostly marine creatures. Of the terrestrial fossils, most are plants. There are not many land-dwelling animals—such as mammals and dinosaurs—found in the fossil record, but the majority of animals depicted on evolutionary fossil charts in textbooks are land vertebrates.

Ammonite

Plants, Including Trees and Algae <5%

<1% Vertebrates of All Kinds

95% Marine Invertebrates, Mostly Shellfish

ALL PHYLA PRESENT AT THE START

If evolution were true, then the fossil record would start with one type of animal life, then increase to two, and so on. Yet fossil studies have shown that essentially all phyla were present at the start, each distinct from the others and each fully equipped to function and survive. Even vertebrate fish were present in the lower Cambrian. This record is what evolutionists call the "Cambrian explosion of life," in which a vast array of animal types suddenly appear. Some of these phyla have gone extinct over subsequent years, but most still live today.

NO ANCESTRY/DESCENDANT RELATIONSHIPS

Evolution necessarily implies the concept of "descent from a common ancestor or ancestors." Yet no ancestor-descendant relationship can be advocated with certainty based on the fossils. In fact, for every proposed transitional form, there is at least one evolutionist who has refuted it on scientific grounds.

Clam

FOSSILS FOUND IN CATASTROPHIC DEPOSITS

Fossil marine creatures are typically found in catastrophic deposits. Even marine creatures that live in high-energy zones cannot live in catastrophic conditions, and many died where they were fossilized. They were either buried alive, or their remains were transported by dynamic processes to their present resting places before they could decay or be scavenged. The processes involved must have been highly destructive and occurred rapidly, unlike the relatively small floods, volcanic eruptions, and other processes of today.

A supposedly 50-million-year-old gar fish fossil looks just like a living gar fish with no sign of evolution.

THE FOSSIL RECORD IS COMPLETE

Charles Darwin was concerned about the fossil record's lack of transitional forms, or hypothetical creatures that demonstrate one type of creature changing into another creature over time. He hoped they would be found one day. But extensive exploration and fossil discovery in the decades since he published his work have not brought such in-between forms to light.

Trilobite

BASIC TYPES SHOW STASIS

Individuals varied in appearance and whole populations varied over the generations to accommodate changing conditions as they "multiplied and filled" Earth's diverse environments. But they were always fundamentally the same as the parent group. If evolutionary descent from a common ancestor were true, then major changes had to have happened in every population, but this is not what we conclude from studying the fossils.

Original Tissue in Fossils

Many paleontologists assume that Earth's rock layers represent millions or billions of years. They have not looked for fresh tissue inside dinosaurs and other fossils because such tissue would have completely mineralized or decayed long ago if the evolutionary timeline were true. But fresh biological material is continually being discovered, despite laboratory data on the biochemistry of molecular decay that clearly show it should not exist after such a long time. Researchers have detected molecules such as proteins, sugars, pigments, and DNA in fossils that are supposedly many millions of years old—as well as intact cells and, in some cases, skin, ligaments, retinas, bones, and blood vessels.

Scientists confirmed partially decayed hemoglobin in the expected positions of this mosasaur's heart and liver. Hemoglobin is a blood protein with a shelf-life of thousands of years. If the fossil really is millions of years old, it would have no hemoglobin left at all.

Several scientific reports of "soft tissue" actually describe tissue that has been partly or totally mineralized. Mineralization occurs when mineral-rich water replaces fragile original tissue, resulting in rocks in the shape of tissue as bone, skin, or other organs. Although some soft tissues are actually mineralized, original tissue fossils also exist. Secular scientists have described original soft tissue fossils from the United States, Argentina, Brazil, England, Germany, Spain, Madagascar, Canada, and at least two Chinese provinces. These tissues should not exist if they are millions of years old. Many more will probably be described in future years, perhaps from even more places. Some may be sitting in museum warehouses even now, waiting to be discovered and analyzed in more depth.

Close-up of mummified skin from hadrosaur fossil below.

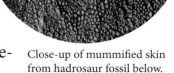

This hadrosaur (called *Trachodon* by Henry F. Osborn in 1912) was discovered by Charles Sternberg in 1908. It is one of the world's best-preserved dinosaurs and came from the Lance Formation of Wyoming. It was given a 68 million-year age assignment, but carbon dates for hadrosaur bones in the Hell Creek Formation in Montana, also said to be 68 million years old, implied an age of 28,790 and 20,850 carbon years. Other discoveries from this formation include original vertebrate proteins from hadrosaur and *T. rex* bones, such as collagen, elastin, PHEX, Histone H4, osteocalcin, and original vertebrate epidermal, red blood, and bone cells (osteocytes).

SKEPTICS

After scientists published the specific amino acid sequence of a dinosaur's collagen protein, other scientists suggested that the sequence was accidentally taken from a modern substance (like someone's lunch) and not from the dinosaur itself. Others have alleged that the proteins found in fossils were manufactured by bacteria. But the kinds of materials produced by bacteria last an even shorter time than proteins that make up vertebrates' bodies. Plus, bacteria do not produce collagen protein, which scientists actually sequenced using multiple and separate labs.

This fossil mosasaur was taken from Niobrara Chalk Formation in western Kansas and dated at 80 million years old. Mosasaurs were marine reptiles whose fossils are found on every continent, including Antarctica. This particular one sat for over 40 years in the Natural History Museum of Los Angeles County before researchers finally tested its chemistry, finding original but partly decayed hemoglobin, still-purple retina cells, and scales (keratin protein). Carbon dating returned an age of 24,600 carbon years before present—a far cry from the original 80 million-year assignment. The study authors said contamination was the cause for this carbon date age, but then they cited evidence that the tissues were original.

LAB TESTS

Laboratory measurements of protein decay rates demonstrate that they can last for thousands of years. One particular protein that can last a long time is collagen inside bone. Collagen is not soluble in water, a property that guards against decay and transport. Collagen still spontaneously decays according to the second law of thermodynamics, which describes how overall randomness always increases. And the warmer the temperature, the more atoms bump into one another to perform more chemistry, accelerating the decay. Rigorous and repeated experiments have shown that bone collagen can last no longer than 700,000 (and likely closer to 450,000) years at 50°F. Its "shelf life" at 70°F is only 2,000 years, which conflicts with its supposed age of 70 to over 100 million years old. And all of the original fossil tissue discoveries are given ages of multiple millions. Clearly, the age assignments for these fossils conflict with their collagen age inferences.

LIMITS

In the case of the paddlefish, mosasaur, and hadrosaur fossils depicted on these pages, two independent scientific tests set upper and lower limits for their ages: 1) Protein shelf life is one million years, assuming perpetual cold since emplacement, and 2) carbon-14 shelf-life is 90,000 years, assuming no carbon-14 has entered or left the system since emplacement. These limits are much younger than the assignments originally given to these fossils.

This paddlefish cartilage fossil from the Green River Formation in Wyoming is supposedly 50 million years old.

Animal	Evolutionary Supposed Age (millions of yrs)	Biochemical Found	Publish Date	Reference
T. rex	68	Collagen	Jun. 2007	Schweitzer, M. Science
Psittacosaurus	125	Collagen	Apr. 2008	Linghan-Soliar, T. Proc. RSB
Brachylophosaurus	80	Elastin	Jul. 2009	Schweitzer, M. Science
Mosasaur	65-68	Hemoglobin	Aug. 2010	Lindgren, J. PLoS ONE
Lizard	40	Keratin	Mar. 2011	Edwards, N. P. Proc. RSB
Mosasaur	70	Collagen	Apr. 2011	San Antonio, J. D. PLoS ONE
Squid	160	Eumelanin	May 2012	Glass, K. PNAS
Scorpion	310	Chitin + protein	Feb. 2011	Cody, G.D. Geology
Lufengosaurus	190	Collagen	Jan. 2017	Lee, Y.-C. N. Comms.

Fossils in this chart likely formed during the year-long Flood of Noah's day. Local catastrophes during the post-Flood Ice Age deposited other soft tissue fossils. Those who insist on millions of years have no credible explanation for these soft tissue discoveries.

Plate Tectonics

Today Earth's surface is divided into tectonic plates that are observed to move relative to one another. The boundaries of these plates are active earthquake zones, allowing us to discern the relative direction of movement.

Plate tectonics was first proposed by creationists in 1860 and adopted by secularists in the 1960s to explain a host of geological and tectonic observations. The secular version of the theory proposes that today's continents drifted into their present positions through subsurface fluid movements transporting the continents at nearly imperceptibly slow speeds. Evidence cited in support of this includes the apparent fit of certain continental coastlines (for example, eastern South America fits the west coast of Africa quite nicely), and the fact that certain faults and linear mountain chains line up when the continents are re-placed together.

While the rate of movement is slow today, only discernible by sensitive satellite-based GPS measuring equipment, scientific evidence has shown that it is likely that in the recent past the plates moved rapidly.

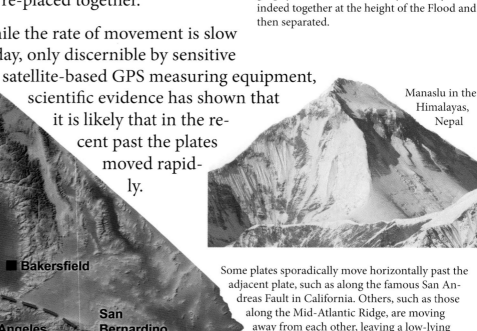

Whether or not the land masses were together at creation, it appears that they were together sometime during the Flood. From matching rock strata traits and boundaries, creationist geophysicists consider it likely that they were indeed together at the height of the Flood and then separated.

Manaslu in the Himalayas, Nepal

Some plates sporadically move horizontally past the adjacent plate, such as along the famous San Andreas Fault in California. Others, such as those along the Mid-Atlantic Ridge, are moving away from each other, leaving a low-lying rift valley between. Some are moving toward each other, and the collisions either crumple up mountains like the Himalayas or cause the more dense oceanic plate to plunge beneath the less dense continental plate, resulting in volcanoes, earthquakes, and occasional tsunamis.

San Andreas Fault in California

CATASTROPHIC PLATE TECTONICS

The tectonic data fit better into the short chronology of Scripture, rather than the long ages of slow movement of the secular hypothesis. Scripture describes the breaking up of the "fountains of the great deep" (Genesis 7:11) as the primary mechanism for not only causing the great Flood and subsequent plate movements, but also ending the Flood and redistributing Earth's land masses to their present configuration.

Evidence shows that the oceanic plates subducted under adjacent continents quite rapidly. Basaltic ocean plates are denser and thus greater in weight than the granitic continents. They would then normally tend to come to rest at a lower elevation. Remnants of the pre-separation continents have actually been discovered deep underground, near the interface of Earth's core and mantle. Some vast cataclysm, like the great Flood, broke them loose and caused them to rapidly sink.

At the height of the Flood, water stood above the mountains. But at its end, the waters rushed off into deep ocean basins, where they are now. Scripture poetically tells us concerning the Flood, "You [God] covered it [Earth] with the deep as with a garment; the waters stood above the mountains. At Your rebuke they fled; at the voice of Your thunder they hastened away. They went up over the mountains; they went down into the valleys, to the place which You founded for them" (Psalm 104:6-8). Some global tectonic mechanism must have been involved to deepen the oceans (the "valleys") and raise the continents.

Plate tectonics no doubt played the major role because as the continents rifted apart, they would have gouged out a low place. This must have involved rapid movements, not the modern miniscule rates. The continents "sprinted" rather than "drifted" to their new locations and left behind low-lying trenches into which the floodwaters drained, thereby exposing the land. The Flood's waters did not need to be removed. They needed only to be redistributed to reveal the land. Concurrently, new oceanic plates formed as basaltic magma rose along the mid-ocean rifts.

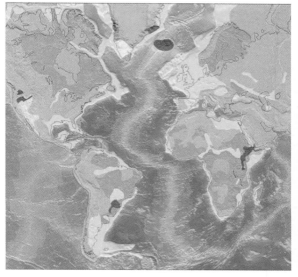

Mantle material rises along fissures between ocean floor plates, like the Mid-Atlantic Ridge illustrated here. At their opposite ends, the plates scoot below less dense continental plates—a process called subduction. Massive ancient volcanoes line continental margins where two plates collided violently and rapidly in the past. The plates once moved many times faster than today.

Apparently, catastrophic plate movements all began with Genesis 7:11, when "all the fountains of the great deep were broken up." Craters deeply buried below rock layers indicate that impacts from outer space probably ruptured Earth's crust, and enormous reservoirs of water mixed with mantle material suddenly surged up through the cracks. Flood processes shoved, tilted, overturned, bent, flattened, buried, elevated, metamorphosed, and melted various Earth materials. Today, geologists detect still-cool subducted ocean plate remnants that were rapidly shoved deep below the surface. If they are millions of years old, why have they not yet warmed up to match the temperature of the hot mantle surrounding them? However, if they were subducted rapidly and recently, as in during the Flood, their present condition makes sense.

The scale of past lava flows dwarfs any we know today. For example, unimaginably large volumes of lava freely flowed from giant fissures in the continental crust, not just from single pipes. The ancient lava flowed so fast that it did not cool or solidify until it had covered broad areas like the Deccan Traps in India, where lava layers have water-deposited sedimentary layers between them. Clearly, the violent earth-restructuring activities of the Flood rapidly formed the Deccan Traps.

Mount St. Helens

To form geologic features, it either takes a little bit of water and a long time or a lot of water and a short time. Even though we did not witness the great Flood of Noah's day, we do see modern catastrophes rapidly accomplish similar things on a much smaller scale. In a short, biblically compatible timescale, such a flood can account for all the major features we see on Earth's surface—features that many geologists normally misinterpret as evidence of long ages. But when the evidence is carefully examined, we see that Earth really is not that old. Instead, we see evidence of a catastrophic event—a worldwide flood.

Floating log mat

When Mount St. Helens erupted in 1980, it allowed us to learn more about volcanism, erosion, deposition, solidification, fossilization, and other phenomena all acting in a short period of time. Although this was a volcanic event, it is in some ways analogous to the Flood. The Mount St. Helens eruption spawned numerous water-related processes and products, since the volcano had once been capped by a thick glacier. Sudden heating melted the ice, causing water to race down the mountain's northern slope. Water moving at a tsunami-like intensity, along with ashfall and pyroclastic flows from the eruption itself, destroyed the forest and hillside below. Some rock quickly eroded, and sediments were deposited in layers that look very similar to layers that secular geologists normally label with very old ages.

Layers of sediments measuring up to 600 feet thick were deposited at the mountain's base in the eruption. These sedimentary layers hardened into solid rock in just a few years. After another few years, canyons were gouged into these layers, producing a smaller scale version of Grand Canyon in just one afternoon.

In other places around Mount St. Helens, other things that supposedly take millions of years happened in just a couple of years. Currently, wood is petrifying and coal is forming.

Hardened pyroclastic flow

LESSONS FROM MOUNT ST. HELENS

- Up to 600 feet of sediments were rapidly deposited, virtually identical to those found worldwide in the greater geologic record.
- A deep, eroded canyon through those sediments, dubbed "Little Grand Canyon," was carved in one afternoon.
- Fresh volcanic rocks called "dacites" are only a few decades old (formed when the volcano erupted). But they were dated by radiometric means to be over a million years old.
- A log mat of about four million trees from a forest that was catastrophically scoured from the ground now floats in a nearby lake.
- A thick peat layer is accumulating under the mat and is poised to become a coal deposit if buried by another eruption.
- Upright floating logs that look like they grew in place have the signature appearance of the "petrified forest" at Yellowstone National Park.

Sedimentary layers with a canyon carved out in one afternoon

The Ice Age

The great Flood of Noah's day drastically changed not just Earth's surface but also its climate. A period characterized by the expansion and advance of high-latitude ice sheets and mountain glaciers followed the Flood. Earth experienced an ice age.

Genesis 7:11 states that at the start of the Flood "all the fountains of the great deep were broken up," meaning that massive amounts of volcanic activity occurred that resulted in climatic impacts lasting for many years after the Flood. The volcanic eruptions heated the oceans and caused evaporation to increase. That resulted in more precipitation, resulting in more snow at the higher latitudes. The Flood's volcanic activity also ejected aerosols (microscopic particles) into the atmosphere, reflecting the sunlight and causing cooler summers that allowed the snow to remain and form glaciers. Aerosols can stay in the air for about six to seven years, but subsequent volcanic activity near or just after the end of the Flood added to those already there. Eventually, when the aerosols tapered off, the sunlight melted much of the ice. During the Ice Age, the ice was thousands of feet thick in some places, and when it melted, the sea level rose.

While the ice sheets covered larger portions of the continents than they do now, the ice didn't cover all of the land. Closer to the equator, the temperatures were more tropical, allowing cold-blooded reptiles like dinosaurs (as well as some warm-blooded creatures) to live and multiply.

Saber-toothed tigers are likely a variety of the felid kind, and their fossils (like those of wooly mammoths) are found in fossil deposits laid down after the Flood. They were colossal animals that were gradually eliminated as mankind spread out across the globe.

MOUNT PINATUBO ERUPTION IN THE PHILIPPINES

Mount Pinatubo is an active volcano on the Philippine island of Luzon. Pinatubo explosively erupted in 1991, spewing aerosols into the atmosphere. A slight atmospheric temperature change occurred after the eruption. This and other explosive eruptions observed in modern history are small compared to the amount and duration of volcanic activity in the great Flood, which was why the Ice Age lasted for a long period and was global in scale.

Wooly rhinoceroses are likely an extinct variety of the rhinoceros kind. A cave in Chauvet, France, contains paintings of wooly rhinoceroses, as well as horses, cattle, mammoths, cave lions, bears, and other animals.

Mammoths were probably a variety of the elephant kind that was represented on the Ark. After the great Flood, there were few predators and plenty of vegetation, allowing them to flourish initially. However, some varieties were eventually overwhelmed in major storms during the Ice Age, while others were hunted to extinction by humans.

Flood Legends from Around the World

Almost every civilization today around the world has a flood legend in its body of folklore. That's because all people alive today descended from the eight people on the Ark. Each account may differ from the others in detail, but the essence of the story remains. Together, they all tell of a prior "golden age" that was destroyed by God due to man's sin. They tell of a faithful, favored family who was warned of the coming flood and who built a large boat and saved themselves and their family.

An image of the building of Noah's Ark from the Nuremberg Chronicle (*Liber Chornicarum*), an illustrated biblical synopsis published in 1493. The characters reflect the medieval dress of the era.

CHRONICLE OF MANASSES

Constantine Manasses was a historian in Byzantium during the 12th century. He authored an illustrated chronicle, or historical synopsis, of events that included the creation of the world, the great Flood and Noah's Ark, the Trojan War, the foundation of Rome, and the reign of several Roman and Byzantine emperors. Manasses, as well as his sponsors and readers, understood that the Flood of Noah's day and other biblical stories were real history.

THE GREAT FLOOD SONG OF THE MIAO PEOPLE

The Miao (also known as the Hmong) is an ethnic minority group, the members of which live in parts of China, Vietnam, Laos, Thailand, and in some countries outside of Asia. The ancient Miao did not keep written records, but they have a long tradition of learning and singing their legends in verse. Those songs include stories of the creation of the world, a great flood in which the survivors escaped in a wooden drum, and a time in which all people spoke one language but were then given many languages and subsequently separated because they could not understand one another. These and many other Miao legends closely parallel the records in the book of Genesis. Their oral traditions include the fact that they descended from *Jah-phu*, or Japheth, the third son of *Nuah* (Noah).

Column capital from the Monastery of Sant Cugat in Sant Cugat del Vallès, Catalonia, Spain. The monastery was founded in the 9th century and completed in the 14th century.

THE FLOOD TABLET FROM THE EPIC OF GILGAMESH

The Epic of Gilgamesh is an epic poem from Mesopotamia about Gilgamesh, a legendary king of the ancient city of Uruk in Sumer (later called Babylonia), and his quest for immortality. The poem was recorded on 12 clay tablets in cuneiform, and one part describes a meeting between Gilgamesh and Utnapishtim, a man who learned of the gods' plan to send a great flood. Like Noah, Utnapishtim built a large boat to save his family, possessions, a host of domesticated and wild animals, and several craftsmen. The flood destroyed mankind, while those aboard the boat survived for six days. The boat landed atop a mountain, and Utnapishtim sent out a number of birds to see if the waters had receded and dry land had appeared again.

HAFIZ-I ABRU'S MAJMA AL-TAWARIKH

Hafiz-i Abru was a Persian historian in the 1400s, and he served under Shah Rukh, the son of Timur the Turkic ruler and founder of the Timurid Dynasty. Under orders from his master, Hafiz-i Abru produced a collection of writings about history and geography, including one about Noah's Ark.

VIRACOCHA

The ancient Incans have a legend in which their creator god, Viracocha, created the earth and the sky, along with several giants. The giants somehow angered Viracocha, so he destroyed them with a great flood, except for one man and one female that survived by floating in a box. Viracocha then made a new race of people from clay to repopulate the earth.

Carbon Dating

Carbon-14, or radiocarbon, dating is a method that scientists use to attempt to determine the age of an object. While we cannot directly assess something's age without some kind of historical record (for example, a birth certificate), carbon dating measures the amount of carbon-14 left in an object. The theory behind the method is that by knowing how much carbon-14 is present, as well as how fast carbon-14 decays, we can know how old something is.

The conflict regarding carbon dating arises when objects such as dinosaur bones, which were originally assigned ages of tens of *millions* of years, possess carbon dates in the tens of *thousands* of years. Since carbon-14 decays so quickly, it shouldn't be present in things that are millions of years old. Yet we constantly find items supposedly that old that still have measurable amounts of carbon-14 in them.

Fossil ammonites and wood found in lower Cretaceous mudstones in California were given ages of 112 to 120 million years. However, carbon-14 testing on fragments from two fossil ammonite shells returned ages between 36,400 and 48,710 carbon years. The carbon ages for the wood were between 32,780 and 42,390 carbon years.

How It Works

Carbon comes in three "varieties" or isotopes—carbon-12, carbon-13, and carbon-14. We know the decay rate of carbon-14—its half-life is 5,730 years. That means that after 5,730 years, half of the amount of carbon-14 in an item would have decayed. After 18 radiocarbon half-lives (or 103,140 years), the amount of carbon-14 in an object would drop below the measurable threshold.

Hadrosaur Bone Test

This bone from a hadrosaur found in the Hell Creek Formation in Montana was originally said to be 68 million years old. When carbon dated, it returned an age of 20,850 carbon years. In other words, the supposedly millions-of-years-old bone still had measurable carbon-14 in it.

Samples from U.S. coal beds, conventionally dated at 40 to 329 million years old, were found to have ages of 48,000 to 50,000 carbon years.

Human remains, like pieces of other once-living organisms, can be carbon tested, and the results can be matched to historical records such as birth certificates or other documentation.

Diamonds are said to be one to two billion years old. However, natural diamonds submitted for radiocarbon analysis had enough carbon-14 still in them to measure. They returned ages of about 55,000 carbon years.

Mummified human remains also contain carbon-14 that can be radiocarbon tested for age. However, we often know the approximate ages of Egyptian mummies because of historical records left behind in the form of engraved hieroglyphics on the tombs in which they are found.

Radiometric Dating

Radiometric, or radioisotope, dating is a method scientists some-times use to calculate the age of rocks. Since geologists cannot directly measure the age of a rock, they choose rocks containing radioactive "parent" isotopes that emit particles (radiation) to become different "daughter" isotopes. They then measure the isotope ratios. Problems arise when scientists attempt to transform these ratios into dates, though, since assigning a date requires the assumption that there was initially no daughter isotope present in the rock, that no isotopes have been added or taken away from the rock, and that the rate at which the parent decays into the daughter has been the same through the rock's history.

A simple illustration can show the problems with these assumptions. Suppose a man hands you a basket with 35 peeled apples. If it normally takes one minute to peel an apple, can you assume the man spent 35 minutes peeling apples? Not necessarily. What if some of the apples were peeled before he got them? What if he spent a longer time and peeled more apples, but ate some of them before giving you the basket? What if some apples took longer to peel than others? In short, while it seems reasonable to assume that the 35 apples represent 35 minutes of peeling, you simply do not know if that's the case unless you were there to witness what happened.

The same goes for measuring the age of a rock. Scientists have observed radioactive isotope (radioisotope) decay rates fluctuating, including Th-228, Rn22, and Si-32. Although these particular isotopes are not used to date rocks, they illustrate that radioisotope decay (radiodecay) is not always constant. Also, rocks that we have observed forming on a particular date often show radioisotope age estimates far exceeding their actual ages. For example, when the fresh lava dome at Mount St. Helens was only ten years old, it showed a radioisotope age estimate of over one million years. Many such examples cast doubt on the entire radiometric dating method.

Radiometric, or radioisotope, dating methods are used to try to find the ages of volcanic rocks. Carbon dating is a completely separate method used to measure the amount of carbon-14 in an organic object, including dinosaur bones and the remains of other once-living things.

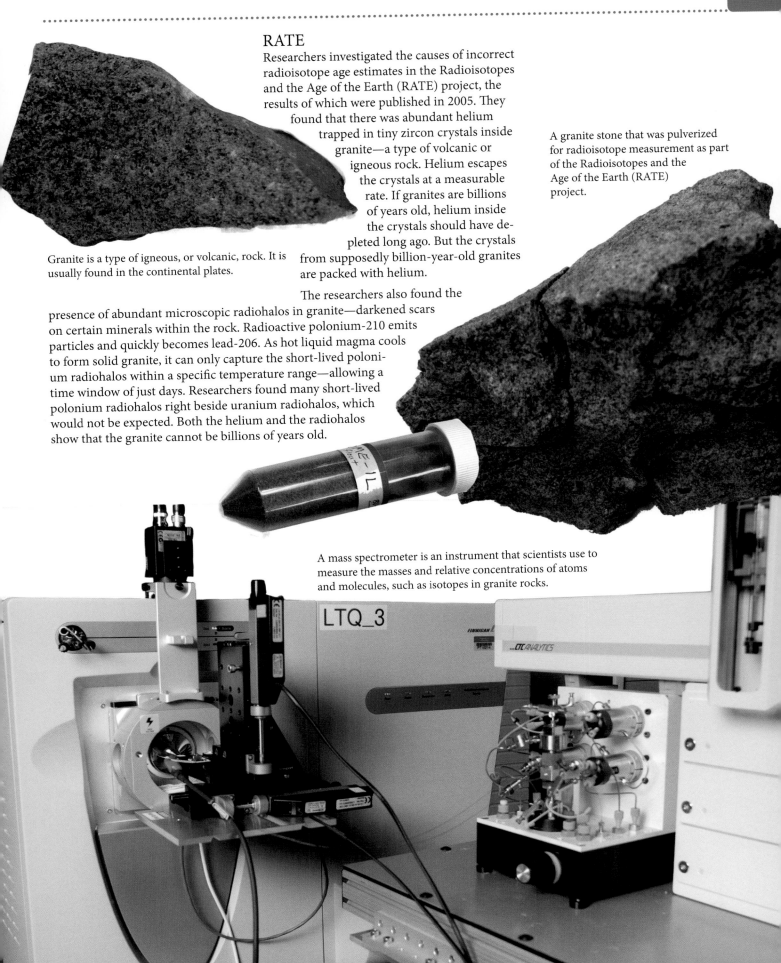

RATE

Researchers investigated the causes of incorrect radioisotope age estimates in the Radioisotopes and the Age of the Earth (RATE) project, the results of which were published in 2005. They found that there was abundant helium trapped in tiny zircon crystals inside granite—a type of volcanic or igneous rock. Helium escapes the crystals at a measurable rate. If granites are billions of years old, helium inside the crystals should have depleted long ago. But the crystals from supposedly billion-year-old granites are packed with helium.

A granite stone that was pulverized for radioisotope measurement as part of the Radioisotopes and the Age of the Earth (RATE) project.

Granite is a type of igneous, or volcanic, rock. It is usually found in the continental plates.

The researchers also found the presence of abundant microscopic radiohalos in granite—darkened scars on certain minerals within the rock. Radioactive polonium-210 emits particles and quickly becomes lead-206. As hot liquid magma cools to form solid granite, it can only capture the short-lived polonium radiohalos within a specific temperature range—allowing a time window of just days. Researchers found many short-lived polonium radiohalos right beside uranium radiohalos, which would not be expected. Both the helium and the radiohalos show that the granite cannot be billions of years old.

A mass spectrometer is an instrument that scientists use to measure the masses and relative concentrations of atoms and molecules, such as isotopes in granite rocks.

THE PHYSICAL
SCIENCES

*"Then God made two great lights:
the greater light to rule the day,
and the lesser light to rule the
night. He made the stars also."*
(Genesis 1:16)

The Laws of Physics Are from God

The Bible teaches that Jesus created everything (John 1). All the matter and energy in our universe came from only one source—God. Matter is the material substance that occupies space, has mass, and is composed predominantly of atoms that consist of protons, neutrons, and electrons. Energy involves motion, or the ability to produce motion. The Bible indicates that Christ upholds the entire universe by the expression of His power (Hebrews 1:3). Every atom is controlled by the Lord, which is why matter and energy behave in a consistent and predictable way. We call these predictable and consistent behaviors the "laws of physics." These laws describe how the fundamental physical qualities of matter and energy act in different circumstances.

The first law of thermodynamics, also known as the law of conservation of energy, states that energy in an isolated system—like our universe—cannot be created or destroyed. It can only be transferred or transformed. This is because God is no longer creating new material (Genesis 2:2), and God upholds what He previously made (Hebrews 1:3, Colossians 1:17). Thermodynamics also deals with a quantity called "entropy." Entropy is a measure of the uselessness of energy. It is a "backward" term because energy that is highly useful has very low entropy and vice versa. The second law of thermodynamics, also known as the law of entropy, states that the entropy of an isolated system that is not in equilibrium, such as the universe, will tend to increase over time. So, although the amount of energy in the universe never changes, its quality is constantly running down.

ISAAC NEWTON

Sir Isaac Newton (1643-1727) is perhaps the most influential scientist of all time. In 1665, he discovered the generalized binomial theorem and began formulating the mathematical theory that would later become calculus. Specializing in mathematics and physics, he became the Lucasian Professor of Mathematics at the University of Cambridge in 1669 and became a member of the prestigious Royal Society in 1671. Though renowned for his scientific pursuits, Newton was a serious student of the Bible and published several theological works. The words "Nature and Nature's laws lay hid in night: God said, Let Newton be! and all was light" appear on his grave in Westminster Abbey in London. The poem was written by English poet Alexander Pope.

Newton's cradle

The swinging pendulum of a clock demonstrates both the first and second laws of thermodynamics. It can only swing when energy is transferred to it from another source to make it move (first law). If it receives no more energy, then it will gradually slow down and eventually stop moving (second law) as its energy is transferred to its surroundings.

Newton conducted a great deal of research in optics and studied the refraction of light—showing how a prism could decompose white light into a color spectrum. This work eventually led to his building of the first known functional reflecting telescope, which is known today as a Newtonian telescope. The transfer refraction of white light into a color spectrum demonstrates the first law of thermodynamics.

Newton's Laws of Motion

Newton formulated three physical laws of motion that are the foundation for classical mechanics. The first law states that an object at rest will stay at rest unless an unbalanced force acts upon it. Likewise, a moving object will continue moving at the same speed and in the same direction unless an unbalanced force acts upon it. This is why we need to wear seatbelts in moving automobiles. If the car suddenly stops, our bodies inside keep moving forward, which causes injury.

The second law states that acceleration occurs when an unbalanced force acts on a mass. If the mass of the object being accelerated is greater, then a greater amount of force is needed to accelerate it. In other words, you may not have trouble kicking a ball, but you will need more force to kick a car to make it move.

Newton's third law of motion is fairly well-known— for every action, there is an equal and opposite reaction. Newton's cradle, decorating some people's desks and bookshelves, illustrates this law.

All three of Newton's laws demonstrate the law of conservation of energy, or the first law of thermodynamics—energy (motion, in this case) in a system cannot be created or destroyed, it can only be transferred.

In 1687, Newton published the first edition of his *Philosophiæ Naturalis Principia Mathematica* (later translated in 1825 as *The Mathematical Principles of Natural Philosophy*), which is considered the single greatest work in the history of science. In the section titled *General Scholium,* he wrote, "This most beautiful system of the sun, planets, and comets, could only proceed from the counsel and dominion of an intelligent and powerful Being.... This Being governs all things, not as the soul of the world, but as Lord over all; and on account of his dominion he is wont to be called *Lord God* "pantokrator," or *Universal Ruler.*"

Problems with the "Big Bang"

How did the universe begin? Some people say, "Well, it sort of exploded into existence, from nothing, billions of years ago. It began in a big bang!"

The Big Bang theory is a popular one, but it does not fit the definition of a scientific theory because it does not make very specific or very numerous predictions about future observations. Also, the Big Bang does not predict any of the observed properties or actions of the universe, such as the relative abundances of the elements, the expansion of the universe, or distribution of galaxies. These things are known (at least approximately), but the Big Bang did not predict them. Instead, it has been retrofitted to accommodate them. The Big Bang is not a scientific theory—it is, instead, a philosophical interpretive framework.

Big Bang proponents conjecture that a universe can spring into existence from a "quantum mechanical fluctuation," or even out of nothing. This has never been observed or confirmed by any experiment. We cannot even think of any way to test the claim.

Horn Antenna at Bell Telephone Laboratories in Holmdel, New Jersey. In 1964, Robert Wilson and Arno Penzias discovered the cosmic microwave background radiation with it, for which they received the 1978 Nobel Prize in Physics.

COSMIC MICROWAVE BACKGROUND RADIATION

Cosmic microwave background (CMB) radiation is a faint source of microwave radiation coming apparently from all directions in space. The Big Bang model predicted that the CMB would have "hot spots" in some places and "cold spots" in others. But observations show the opposite—the CMB is very uniform, with only slight temperature fluctuations. Current Big Bang models have been adjusted to match the observed CMB, which is often the case when new discoveries contradict the model. But adjusting a model to accommodate evidence is not good science, particularly when it is adjusted multiple times like the Big Bang has been.

THE FLATNESS PROBLEM

Redshift happens when light from an object that is moving away is proportionally increased in wavelength, or shifted to the red end of the visible spectrum. Observations of the redshifts of galaxies indicate that the universe is apparently expanding. On the other hand, galaxies also have gravity, which (if it were not for expansion) would cause them to move closer to each other and make the universe smaller. Gravity and expansion oppose each other, and it happens that they are very finely balanced—almost perfectly. Yet, according to the Big Bang, this perfect balance was somehow achieved by an accidental, uncaused "explosion."

THE HORIZON PROBLEM

According to the Big Bang model, the universe started out very small with large temperature fluctuations from place to place—"hot spots" and "cold spots." But the distant universe seems to have the same temperature everywhere, with only minor fluctuations. If you put an ice cube (a "cold spot") in hot coffee (a "hot spot"), you will eventually end up with luke-warm coffee. Energy naturally moves from hot areas to cold areas. But even moving at the speed of light, there has not been enough time (even if we accept the Big Bang's timescale of 13.8 billion years) for the energy to travel from the hot spots to the cold spots to "even out" the temperatures.

THE MONOPOLE PROBLEM

Magnets always have two "poles"—a north pole and a south pole. A magnetic monopole is a hypothetical particle that has only one magnetic pole. According to our current understanding of physics, these particles should be produced at extremely high temperatures—the kinds of temperatures that would have occurred during the Big Bang. Yet not a single monopole has ever been discovered.

INFLATION

When secular scientists were confronted with the flatness, horizon, and monopole problems with the Big Bang, the model was retrofitted somewhat to accommodate them. This new addition is called "inflation" because it suggests that the universe briefly underwent a period of accelerated expansion (the inflation phase) shortly after the moment of the Big Bang. Then the inflation turned off and the universe went back to its normal expansion rate—at least for our region of the universe. But inflation amounts to nothing more than additional assumptions, and it has problems of its own. What would cause the inflation? What would stop it? How could it be stopped everywhere at the same time (the "graceful exit problem")? In addition, there are other problems with the Big Bang that would not be solved even if inflation were true.

NOTHING?

THE BARYON NUMBER PROBLEM

The universe contains very little antimatter, which is identical to ordinary matter except that the charges of the particles are reversed. (Antiprotons have a negative charge.) The Big Bang model maintains that the early universe was made up only of energy. It was too hot for matter. As the universe expanded and cooled, some of the energy transformed into the ordinary matter we have today. It is possible to make matter from energy because this can be repeated in particle accelerators. However, every time we make matter from energy, we get a precisely equal amount of antimatter. If the Big Bang were true and all the matter in the universe came from energy, there should be an exactly equal amount of antimatter. But there is not.

DISTANT MATURE GALAXIES

As we build increasingly powerful telescopes and peer into distant regions of the universe, we continue to find galaxies of magnificent beauty and complexity. This is perfectly consistent with biblical creation, but it is a problem for the Big Bang. Such galaxies should not exist at such distances because these distances are supposed to represent times in the early universe before galaxies would have had a chance to form.

Recent Creation of Our Solar System

Our solar system consists of our star, the sun, and a system of planets, their moons, and other non-stellar objects such as asteroids and comets. The terrestrial planets, Mercury, Venus, Earth, and Mars, are mostly made of rock and metal. The other planets—Jupiter, Saturn, Uranus, and Neptune—are mostly composed of gases or "ices" (substances with relatively high melting points). Pluto was considered the ninth planet in our solar system until it was recategorized as a dwarf planet in 2006.

The solar system is located about two-thirds of the way to the edge of the Milky Way galaxy. Most of the stars in our galaxy are in the larger spiral arms or in the center. Because there are few stars near us, our solar system has a low amount of radiation surrounding it, and we can observe the rest of the universe and our own galaxy much better.

Secular scientists believe that our solar system formed 4.6 billion years ago through unguided natural processes. However, almost every part of our system demonstrates that it was created purposefully and recently.

MERCURY
The closest planet in our solar system to the sun is Mercury. It is also the smallest planet, and it orbits the sun about once every 88 Earth days. Most planets, including Earth, generate magnetic fields that encompass the space around them. Every planet's magnetic field is breaking down as time goes by, but Mercury's is fading extremely fast. In fact, recent measurements found that its field strength decayed by 4 percent in just 33 years. If Mercury was billions (or even just millions) of years old, its magnetic field would have disappeared long ago, along with the magnetic fields of all the other planets.

ENCELADUS
Enceladus is Saturn's sixth-largest moon, and it is a most unusual part of our solar system. The German-born British astronomer William Herschel discovered it in 1789. It is the brightest object in the solar system, reflecting nearly all the light that hits it. NASA images of Enceladus show many plumes of water being ejected with great force, similar to geysers here on Earth. When the water is ejected, it freezes immediately, creating the plumes that we see. Clearly, Enceladus is very active, which means it has a lot of energy and cannot be as old as secularists claim.

Johann Kepler: Father of Physical Astronomy

Johann Kepler (1571-1630) was an astronomer who lived during the time the Holy Roman Empire ruled Germany. As a boy, he observed the Great Comet of 1577 and the Lunar Eclipse of 1580, which no doubt fueled his curiosity and enthusiasm for science. After studying mathematics and astronomy in Austria, he assisted Tycho Brahe, the court mathematician to Emperor Rudolf II. Upon Tycho's death, Kepler inherited his position, as well as his extensive archive of planetary observations. Kepler is best known for discovering the three mathematical laws of planetary motion (Kepler's Laws) that established the discipline of celestial mechanics. He also discovered the elliptical patterns in which the planets travel around the sun. At a time when the sun and other celestial bodies were still widely believed to circle Earth (geocentrism), Kepler defended Nicolaus Copernicus' theory that planets orbit the sun (heliocentrism) and sought to reconcile it with current theology. He revolutionized scientific thought by applying physics (then considered a branch of natural philosophy) to astronomy (seen as a branch of mathematics). In Kepler's view, the universe itself was an image of God, with the sun corresponding to the Father, the stellar sphere to the Son, and the intervening space to the Holy Spirit.

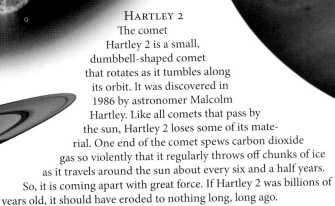

Hartley 2
The comet Hartley 2 is a small, dumbbell-shaped comet that rotates as it tumbles along its orbit. It was discovered in 1986 by astronomer Malcolm Hartley. Like all comets that pass by the sun, Hartley 2 loses some of its material. One end of the comet spews carbon dioxide gas so violently that it regularly throws off chunks of ice as it travels around the sun about every six and a half years. So, it is coming apart with great force. If Hartley 2 was billions of years old, it should have eroded to nothing long, long ago.

Internal Heat of Giant Planets
Jupiter gives off about twice the amount of energy that it receives from the sun. But Jupiter only has a finite amount of energy, so it cannot do this forever. If it was 4.6 billion years old, as secular astronomers claim, it would be a dead and cold planet now. The problem is even more challenging for Neptune, which emits 2.7 times the amount of energy that it receives from the sun. Neptune is large enough that it can do this for thousands of years—but not billions. Uranus (which is essentially the same size, mass, and composition as Neptune) does not have this excess internal heat. This is perplexing from a secular point of view, since these planets allegedly formed at the same time under nearly identical circumstances.

Rings of Saturn
Saturn is the second-largest planet in our solar system, after Jupiter. It is called a "gas giant" because it is mostly made up of helium and hydrogen. Many people know Saturn because of its spectacular system of rings that are composed mostly of ice, rocky debris, and dust. Saturn's rings look youthful for a variety of reasons. For one, they are bright and shiny. After millions of years, the icy rings should have collected so much space dust that they would look like charcoal now. Also, the small moons embedded among the rings should have been flung away long ago. Because Saturn's rings look like they were recently created, it is reasonable to think that Saturn and the rest of our solar system was also recently created.

"When I consider Your heavens, the work of Your fingers, the moon and the stars, which You have ordained, what is man that You are mindful of him, and the son of man that You visit him?" (Psalm 8:3-4)

The size of Earth in relation to the sun and other planets of our solar system

Arcturus

Sun

Sirius

Pollux

The sun in relation
to other stars

Recent Creation of the Universe

Secular scientists maintain that Earth is 4.6 billion years old and that the universe is 13.8 billion years old. However, those billions-of-years age estimates are not based primarily on science, and we are usually not told about the evidence indicating that the universe is much younger than billions of years.

Unfortunately, the methods of science do not allow us to actually measure age as we would measure something like mass or composition. Age is not a substance that can be detected in a laboratory. At best, we can make an educated guess about when a particular process began by knowing 1) its initial state and 2) its rate of change. The only thing we can actually measure in the present is the rate of change today, since the rate of change of any process may have been different in the past.

The three stars making up the "belt" of the Orion constellation are blue stars.

Furthermore, we can never really know the initial state because we were not there when the process began. Despite these difficulties, we can still make an estimation of the maximum age of a system (even if the initial condition is unknown) because in many cases the initial condition cannot be outside of a certain range. For example, we may not know the initial amount of salt in the ocean, but we can know for certain that it cannot be less than zero percent. You can't have less salt than no salt!

Spiral Galaxies

Spiral galaxies are comprised of hundreds of billions of stars organized into "arms" that are twisted around the disk. Their inner regions rotate faster than the outer regions, so the spiral structure must necessarily get slightly "tighter" every year. The rotation rate is slow enough that the spiral structure could persist for as long as 100 million years. But once we get to a billion years, the spiral arms would be twisted beyond recognition, and the disk would be a uniform blend.

Still, secular astronomers think spiral galaxies are 10 billion years old, and they proposed that a process within the galaxies creates new arms as old ones are twisted together. However, it is well known in physics that plasma (ionized gas) can only move parallel to the direction of the magnetic fields that parallel the spiral arms. Therefore, spiral arms (which contain a great deal of plasma) and their magnetic fields must rotate together (differentially). So when a new spiral arm is supposedly created, it would not align with the original (now highly twisted) magnetic field. That is contrary to our observations.

The Pinwheel Galaxy (M101) is a spiral galaxy located in the constellation Ursa Major. This image combines infrared, visible, ultraviolet, and X-ray data from four NASA space telescopes.

Blue Stars

Most stars generate energy through the process of nuclear fusion of hydrogen into helium in the stellar core. Theoretically, a star like the sun has enough hydrogen to keep burning for 10 billion years. But that is not the case with blue stars, which are always more massive than the sun. This means they have more hydrogen available as fuel. Yet, blue stars are much brighter than the sun (some are over 200,000 times brighter), and they "burn" their fuel much more quickly than the sun. Therefore, they cannot last billions of years. And based on their observed luminosity, the most massive blue stars cannot last even one million years before running out of fuel. If the universe was 13.8 billion years old, as secularists claim, blue stars should not be here anymore.

(Above) Bode's Galaxy (M81) is a spiral galaxy in the constellation Ursa Major. It has been studied extensively by professional astronomers due to its proximity to Earth, large size, and active galactic nucleus.

(Left) The Whirlpool Galaxy (M51a) is a spiral galaxy in the constellation Canes Venatici. It is a popular study subject for professional astronomers wanting to understand more about galaxy structure.

(Right) The Pleiades, or Seven Sisters, is a cluster of blue stars located in the constellation Taurus. It is one of the closest star clusters to Earth and can be seen without a telescope at night.

Out of Place in Outer Space

Every one of the universe's countless luminaries shines with a unique light, spins in a unique direction, or interacts with unique stellar partners in a unique location. In short, outer space is filled with phenomena that are out of place for nature-only explanations, which is what we would expect to see based on Scripture: "One star differs from another star in glory" (1 Corinthians 15:41). "I have made the earth, and created man on it. I—My hands—stretched out the heavens, and all their host I have commanded" (Isaiah 45:12).

No Star Formation

Any star is actually out of place in outer space. Though secular reports routinely point out areas of "star formation" and refer to star "nurseries," nobody has yet reported a newly formed star. In fact, the laws of physics strongly resist star formation from gas clouds, which is the usual explanation. One way to potentially overcome the repulsive forces between gas particles is for shockwaves from a nearby star explosion to squeeze the gas so tightly together that their gravity begins to hold it. But then, how would the first star ever have formed? However, the difficulties with natural star formation do not plague the idea of supernatural star formation—"By the word of the LORD the heavens were made, and all the host of them by the breath of His mouth" (Psalm 33:6).

Quasars

Naturalistic Big Bang cosmology assumes that matter is distributed evenly over large scales and that no unique places exist within the cosmos. Neither assumption finds support from space features like super-bright, super-massive, quasi-stellar radio sources (quasars). Instead, a massive network of quasars discovered in 2013 spanned a stretch of space four times larger than the maximum "large scale" range that Big Bang allowed. The Lord placed these quasar mega-structures right where He wanted them.

Galaxies Are Too Far Away

Nature-only origins ideas suggest that objects found in the most distant reaches of space are billions of years younger than more nearby objects. Those found far away should look like baby galaxies if the Big Bang is true, but they do not. Astronomers continually discover "mature" galaxies in "young" places. For example, the Abell 383 galactic cluster's gravitational lens brings into view a galaxy ordinarily too distant for our most powerful telescopes to register. The apparently mature galaxy sits in supposedly immature space. These observations fit well with the Bible's assertion that God recently created space and all its luminaries—both near and far.

Missing Supernova Remnants

A supernova happens when a star explodes after becoming unstable from burning too much of its own fuel. Its explosion leaves behind a glowing gas cloud called "supernova remnants." If the universe is billions of years old, we should see many of these remnants. But according to the number of observed supernova remnants and the rate of supernova occurrences, astronomers estimate that only about 7,000 years' worth of supernovas has occurred.

Starlight and Time

Galaxies have been detected at distances of several billion light-years. Since a light-year (equal to about 6 trillion miles) is the distance that light travels in one year, it would seem that the light from these distant galaxies must have been produced billions of years ago in order to reach Earth today. But this is contrary to the biblical timescale, as well as other scientific data that indicate the universe is about 6,000 years old. Many of the proposed answers to the starlight paradox are not realistic. But there is a solution based on standard physics that shows starlight can indeed reach Earth from the farthest galaxies in virtually no time at all.

Theoretical physicist Albert Einstein (1879-1955) concluded that velocity affects the passage of time and the measurement of distances. Specifically, clocks tick slower when they are moving (relative to an observer) than when they are stationary, and lengths contract in the direction of motion when the object is moving. These effects seem strange to us because they are so tiny at the velocities we normally travel that we cannot detect them. And since we do not notice, we tend to assume that motion has no effect on time or space. But the effects are there, and they become very large at velocities close to the speed of light.

Theoretical physicist Albert Einstein is famous for developing the general theory of relativity, which along with quantum mechanics is considered one of the two pillars of modern physics.

THE ONE-WAY SPEED OF LIGHT

Another well-established (though not commonly known) implication of relativity is that the speed of light in a vacuum can be objectively measured only on a round trip. It cannot be measured on a one-way trip without first assuming this speed. Suppose we had access to a hallway that was 186,282.397 miles long, and we place a mirror at one end and a clock and flashlight at the other. We could measure the speed of light by turning on the flashlight exactly when the clock strikes noon and then recording the time when the beam returns back to the clock. We would find it takes exactly two seconds for the beam to travel to the end of the hallway, reflect off the mirror, and return to its source. Dividing the total distance (twice the length of the hall-way) by the total time (two seconds) gives us the speed of light: 186,282.397 miles per second (which is 670,616,629 mph).

But this is a time-averaged speed, and there is no guarantee that the light travelled this speed the entire trip. Perhaps the light took only a half-second to reach the mirror and 1.5 seconds to return. Or, perhaps the light took two seconds to reach the mirror and travelled back instantaneously. Our experiment only gives us the two-way (round-trip) average speed of light.

To measure the speed of light on a one-way path, we would need a clock at both ends of the hallway—one to measure when the beam of light starts and the other for when the beam reaches the other end of the hallway. And since we know the distance, we can compute the one-way speed of light, right? Well, no, because Clock 2 may be one second slow ("behind" Clock 1), in which case the light really took two seconds to traverse the distance. Or perhaps Clock 2 is one second fast, in which case the light took no time at all to traverse the distance. In order for us to actually know the one-way speed of light, the two clocks must be precise-ly synchronized—a seemingly simple task that is remarkably difficult to achieve. Physicists have shown that two clocks separated by a distance can only be synchro-nized if the one-way speed of light is known in advance. So, we would have to first know the one-way speed of light in order to synchronize clocks so that we could then measure the one-way speed of light. But we cannot know the one-way speed of light unless we first measure it.

Einstein realized this dilemma and concluded that the one-way speed of light is not actually a property of nature but is, instead, a convention that is stipulated by human beings. A convention is something that we decide on and then use to measure other things (e.g., 12 inches = 1 foot). There is no prop-erty of the universe that forces 12 inches to be a foot. We made that decision. Likewise, Einstein decided for simplicity to make the one-way speed of light the same in all directions, but he agreed that other choices were equally valid. Therefore, we can choose the speed of light to be instantaneous when moving toward an observer, eliminating any perceived distant starlight problem.

WHAT THE BIBLE SAYS ABOUT STARLIGHT

The Bible implies that starlight took time to arrive on Earth. Genesis 1:14-15 states, "Then God said, 'Let there be lights in the firmament of the heavens to divide the day from the night; and let them be for signs and seasons, and for days and years; and let them be for lights in the firmament of the heavens to give light on the earth'; and it was so." This indicates that the lights in the sky, which include the stars (Genesis 1:16), were made "to give light on the earth." The text also states "and it was so," affirming that the stars did indeed give light upon Earth instantly, or at least that day. Moreover, ancient cultures did not subtract light-travel times from celestial events.

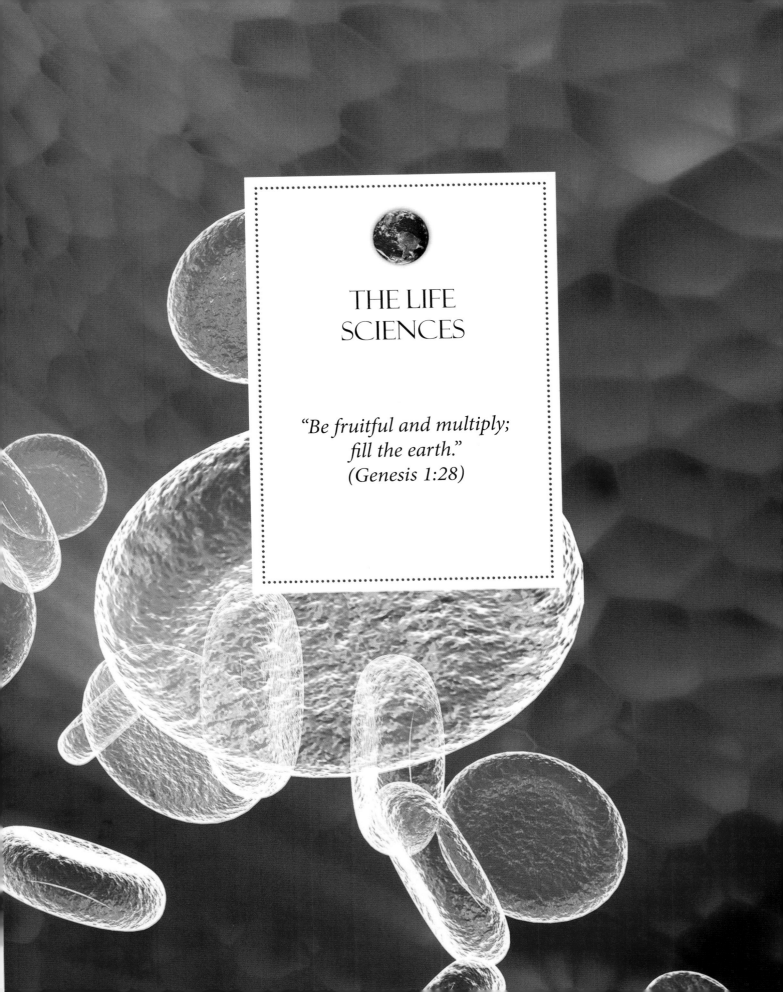

THE LIFE SCIENCES

"Be fruitful and multiply;
fill the earth."
(Genesis 1:28)

Life's All-or-Nothing Design

"All-or-nothing" means that without all of a system's vital parts, the system would not function. These kinds of systems clearly demonstrate created design because all of the vital parts had to have been fashioned, fixed in place, and set in motion at one time. Removing a single vital component would cause the system to stop functioning. In essence, the first cells and creatures must have been created, since it is not possible for their parts to have arrived piecemeal and randomly the way secular naturalists insist.

Also, the core set of body or cell parts in all-or-nothing living systems cannot withstand being rearranged in the ways that molecules-to-man evolution teaches. For example, a dinosaur can never evolve into a bird because the bird's flow-through lung design would have to replace the reptilian bellows lung design. Dinosaurs could never have held their breath for thousands of generations while waiting on natural processes to swap out lung systems bit by bit. God made the first of each all-or-nothing living system instantly: "For He spoke, and it was done; He commanded, and it stood fast" (Psalm 33:9).

YUCCA PLANT AND YUCCA MOTH

Most plants can be pollinated by a variety of insects, and most insects can use different plants to meet their needs. However, the yucca plant does not survive without the yucca moth, also called the pronuba moth, and vice versa. In the process of depositing its eggs among the yucca plant's seed cells, the moth pollinates the yucca flowers. Pronuba larvae eat only some of the yucca seeds as they mature. The plant supplies vital food and a nursery to the moth, and the moth enables the yucca to produce the next generation. Clearly, this plant and moth were designed to live together.

ALL-OR-NOTHING DESIGN BETWEEN DIFFERENT SPECIES

God designed many animals to depend on very different creations, such as a specific plant or bacterium. The termite, for example, depends on microbes living in its gut that can digest wood. In turn, the termite's gut supplies the microbes with their required environment and nutrients.

VITAL VS. NON-VITAL COMPONENTS

Most machines use interacting parts that fit together just right, and the biological machines that support cells, whole organisms, and even Earth's ecosystems are no exceptions. Some parts are absolutely necessary, but others are not. For example, a car without an engine or wheels would be useless steel, glass, and plastic. But without its radio antenna or exterior paint, a car would still get you places. In the same way, your body would not work without a minimum set of its total parts, like its lungs, liver, or lymph nodes. But the body will not necessarily die if it loses a finger, patella, or pancreas. The minimum required parts make up the vital all-or-nothing design of that machine, whether it is made by humans or by God.

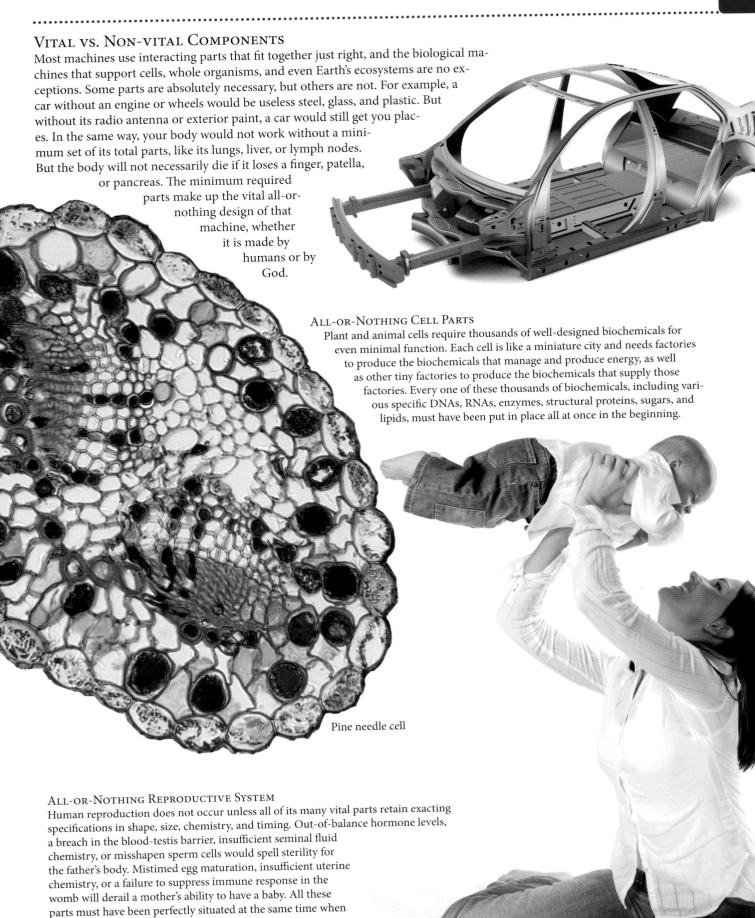

ALL-OR-NOTHING CELL PARTS

Plant and animal cells require thousands of well-designed biochemicals for even minimal function. Each cell is like a miniature city and needs factories to produce the biochemicals that manage and produce energy, as well as other tiny factories to produce the biochemicals that supply those factories. Every one of these thousands of biochemicals, including various specific DNAs, RNAs, enzymes, structural proteins, sugars, and lipids, must have been put in place all at once in the beginning.

Pine needle cell

ALL-OR-NOTHING REPRODUCTIVE SYSTEM

Human reproduction does not occur unless all of its many vital parts retain exacting specifications in shape, size, chemistry, and timing. Out-of-balance hormone levels, a breach in the blood-testis barrier, insufficient seminal fluid chemistry, or misshapen sperm cells would spell sterility for the father's body. Mistimed egg maturation, insufficient uterine chemistry, or a failure to suppress immune response in the womb will derail a mother's ability to have a baby. All these parts must have been perfectly situated at the same time when God created the first father and mother, Adam and Eve.

Interdependence in Living Things

Living things require other living things in order to survive. We easily observe the interdependence between living things in nature the same way we observe the interdependence of man-made systems, like companies. Without all the necessary components functioning well and working efficiently, the system breaks down. Biological interdependence is therefore a product of design, not chance.

"But now ask the beasts, and they will teach you; and the birds of the air, and they will tell you; or speak to the earth, and it will teach you; and the fish of the sea will explain to you. Who among all these does not know that the hand of the Lord *has done this, in whose hand is the life of every living thing, and the breath of all mankind?" (Job 12:7-10)*

The world's land and ocean plants and animals all participate in an interdependent web requiring many different parts. Contrary to popular notions of a fragile earth atmosphere, an array of microbes constantly maintains the world's crucially balanced levels of atmospheric gases like methane, carbon dioxide, oxygen, and nitrogen.

Various organisms play crucial roles to support their ecosystems, including the cycling of nutrients, energy, and wastes. Animals and most other living forms generate carbon dioxide that plants use to build sugars during photosynthesis. And, of course, some of those same plants produce the oxygen and food that fuel all other animal life. Plants and animals were made for each other.

Cells—Worlds of Activity Too Small to See

The inner workings of the cell point toward God's design like nothing else in biology. Genesis 1:1 states, "In the beginning God created the heavens and the earth." Before the universe was, it existed only in His mind. Therefore, He alone knows everything about every molecule in every place. The way He intended each creation is exactly how it became. There were no mistakes, prototypes, or second tries when God designed living things.

The minimum requirements for physical cellular life are vast in number, information-rich, and precise in structure. Natural processes are not known to generate any of the kinds of molecular machines—many of which can manipulate specific, single atoms—that are required to sustain cells. And the laws of chemistry and physics alone could not manufacture the very mechanisms that enable living things to minimize the natural consequences of those laws—decay and diffusion. The higher the number of specifications required for life, the lower the probability that life could have arisen through random, undirected forces. The actual number of specifications now known is so high that there is no reasonable doubt that life must have been engineered by a perceptive power that exists beyond natural laws. Since natural entities cannot account for life, a supernatural entity must. The cell bears remarkable testimony to God's goodness and supreme intelligence in creating biological creatures that are made of cells.

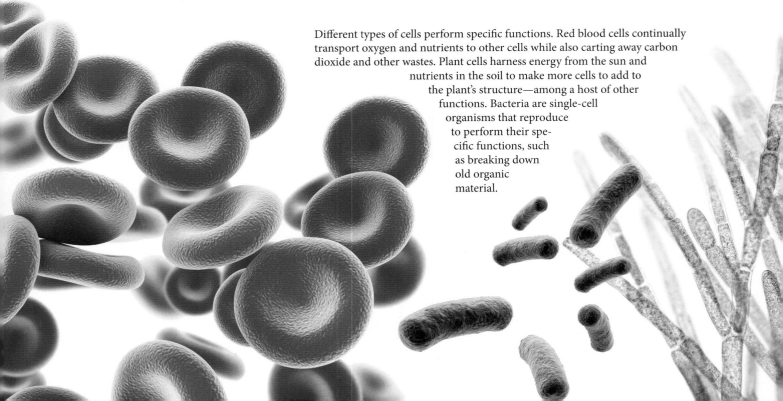

Different types of cells perform specific functions. Red blood cells continually transport oxygen and nutrients to other cells while also carting away carbon dioxide and other wastes. Plant cells harness energy from the sun and nutrients in the soil to make more cells to add to the plant's structure—among a host of other functions. Bacteria are single-cell organisms that reproduce to perform their specific functions, such as breaking down old organic material.

BUILDING A COMPLEX STRUCTURE

Despite being microscopic, cells are complex structures that require sophisticated machinery in order to function properly. Four steps required in the construction of a complex structure, such as an automobile, need intelligent intervention. First, the energy and raw materials must be converted into useful forms, sizes, and shapes (e.g., electricity, steel or aluminum ore, petroleum for plastic, rubber for tires, gasoline refinery, etc.) before they can participate in the construction process. Second, the transformed energy and materials need to be assembled. Third, that assembly must follow a specific blueprint or plan that was developed beforehand. A plan also ensures that just enough raw materials are gathered, reducing waste and increasing efficiency. Finally, the plan is enforced by someone who can read, interpret, and execute the plan. The same goes for cells in building complex structures like people, plants, and animals. Cells must 1) transform energy and raw materials into something useful for cell growth, 2) harness the energy to do useful work, 3) organize the work according to a plan, and 4) enforce the plan.

FAR FROM SIMPLE

Cells maintain their own miniature power plants called mitochondria in which tiny protein machines harvest the energy present in chemical bonds of energy-rich sugars obtained from food. It adds that energy to adenosine triphosphate (ATP), which is like the electricity that most machines and tools inside cells are designed to run on. Cells also manufacture building blocks according to stringent quality control standards and in accordance with the needs of the relevant project (too little or too much material would be inefficient or fatal). Much of the work in cells is performed by two major types of "tools"—proteins and RNA, both of which are involved in everything from fat synthesis to cell division to information processing. The cells also organize the work according to the "blueprint" found in DNA. And finally, the cell enforces the plan when the RNA and proteins read and translate the DNA-encoded plan to make just the right components in just the right amounts at just the right time. Thus, cells are very complex and efficient systems.

CELL DIVISION

Cells can take from 20 minutes to 24 hours to divide, depending on their type. Imagine constructing a complete and fully functional space shuttle every 20 minutes continually. That would still not be on par with the level of complexity and efficiency at which cells operate.

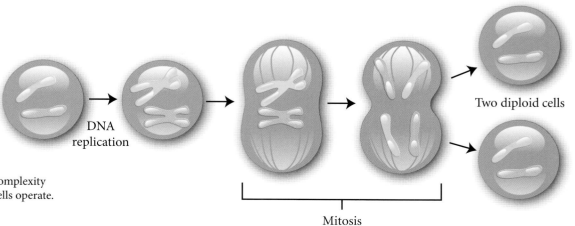

DNA replication

Mitosis

Two diploid cells

Creature Changes

Do species change? Evolution is founded on the assumption that any species can change into any other species, given enough time. What do we observe?

Field observations and laboratory experiments around the world tell a consistent story. Variety within and between creatures is abundant, and change continually occurs as species respond to changing environments. However, no large-scale evolutionary changes have ever been witnessed.

Every example of "evolutionary" change in the field or in the lab depicts variation within biblical limits. Scripture limits the ancestry of each species to a created "kind" of Genesis 1, and all species' changes occur within "kinds." No exceptions to this rule have ever been found. Biological observations confirms the text of Genesis.

STICKLEBACK FISH
In separate generations, stickleback fish can change from being able to live in fresh water to living in salt water and then back. However, the stickleback fish still remains a stickleback fish.

COLOR VARIATION
Foxes with different coat colors exist in different environments. Where did this variety come from? Their Creator programmed it into the genetic code of their forebears, which probably looked like today's wolf.

BODY SIZE

Foxes and wolves both come from the canine kind. Their difference in size is a variation within the kind, not an evolutionary change.

LAND AND SEA

Different species of iguanas are uniquely adapted to land and marine environments. Yet, they can interbreed, showing that they came from the same kind.

FINCH BEAKS

Charles Darwin used variations in finch beaks to illustrate how all creatures might have developed from a common ancestor through eons of gradual changes. However, the beak changes are small (unlike arms changing into wings, for instance). In addition, all the Galapagos finch species likely belonged to the same kind. Even this textbook example of "evolution" is a demonstration of biblical variation.

Cactus finch

Ground finch

Variation Within a Kind

The term "species" never occurs in Scripture. The biblical text repeatedly uses the Hebrew word *min*, translated as "kind" in most English Bibles, to describe biological life. *Min* appears 31 times in Scripture—in the creation and Flood accounts (Genesis 1, 6–7), in the Mosaic law (Leviticus 11, Deuteronomy 14), and once in the Prophets (Ezekiel 47). The use of *min* in these contexts reveals profound insights to species' origin.

In Genesis 1, *min* denotes a created category of creature. For example, in Genesis 1:25, "God made the beast of the earth according to its kind, cattle according to its kind, and everything that creeps on the earth according to its kind." In Genesis 6:19, God commands Noah to take "male and female" of each kind on board the Ark. Apparently, individuals within a kind can breed only with other members of the same kind—in other words, reproductive boundaries define the limits of each kind. Thus, members of the same kind can be recognized by their ability to interbreed. In addition, God blessed creatures to multiply and fill the earth, so today's species are descendants from the original created kinds.

Pine trees and rose plants cannot interbreed because they belong to two different plant kinds.

Like kinds beget like kinds, so wood frogs only produce more frogs. They cannot produce creatures from other kinds, like fish or rabbits.

LIMITS TO VARIATION

Scripture implies that kinds cannot be interconverted (one changed into another), that there is a limit to biological change and speciation. As a general rule, the limit corresponds to the family level in most cases, not species. The barrier to kind interconversion is implied by God's command to take two of every land air-breathing kind to "keep seed alive upon the face of all the earth" (Genesis 7:3, KJV). If one of the land kinds had failed to board the Ark, it would have died in the Flood and had no offspring—extinction! If kinds could be interconverted, there would have been no need to load every land kind on the Ark—just a few would have sufficed, and all those kinds not boarding the Ark could have been recovered via interconverting the kinds on the Ark after the Flood. But as both Scripture and scientific observation demonstrate, there is a hard limit to speciation and to biological change, and that means all living things descending from a common ancestor is impossible.

These leaves from holly plants belong to the same kind (*min* in Hebrew) because they can interbreed to produce varieties within their kind. They cannot breed with non-holly trees.

What differences and similarities do you notice in these holly plants?

ONE "TREE" VS. MANY TREES

Phylogenetic techniques (using evolutionary "trees" inspired by Darwin) show proposed evolutionary relationships between living things. However, the trees are often incorrect because they attempt to show common ancestry between separated kinds. Tracing the relationships between all living things is impossible. Tracing the relationships between members of the same kind is feasible. For instance, horses, donkeys, and zebras can interbreed, so they belong to the same kind—equids. Cats, tigers, ligers, and lions belong to the felid kind. There is no connection between the equid "tree" and felid "tree." Hence, there is no common ancestor between these two kinds.

Variation Within Swallowtail Butterflies

Swallowtail butterflies comprise a "tribe" or "supergenus" named Papilionini, which consists of 203 species worldwide. They almost all have a narrow "flute" that extends backward from the rear wings, like the swallowtail bird. Each species is distinguished by where it lives, how it looks, and which particular plant its larvae (called caterpillars) eat.

Although more research is needed to verify this, it is quite possible that all of today's swallowtail butterfly varieties are descendants of the first of this "kind" that were made during creation week.

Swallowtails illustrate the concept of variation within a kind. Certain processes like genetic recombination, gene transposition, and epigenetic patterning serve to generate varieties between generations in many animals, and may have been involved in generating swallowtail variations—including caterpillar food preferences—since creation.

Biomimicry—Humans Copying God's Design

The design features that God programmed into natural systems are so finely tuned that they are used as models for human inventors to follow. Some natural systems, especially living systems, contain ingenious solutions for solving technical problems. Humans must solve the same physical problems to achieve similar results, and we often take inspiration from pre-existing devices found in nature. This practice, called biomimicry, ranges from the simple to the complex.

Evolutionary philosophy holds that ingenious biological features were invented by the unknowing, uncaring, purposeless laws of nature, but it is clear that they were instead engineered by our wise, benevolent, and powerful Creator. Nature has never been observed inventing these kinds of complex structures—each well-suited to its task—and there is not even a theoretical, realistic, step-by-step evolutionary explanation for how they could have developed. Thus, in the same way that we infer a painter from a painting or an engineer from an engine, we infer a Creator from a creation.

HUMAN HANDS

The human hand is undeniably a work of wonder. Its layout and suite of design features enable mankind—the only possessors of this particular arrangement of bones, tendons, muscles, and nerves—to type faster than 60 words per minute or swing a heavy hammer while holding a delicate potato chip. Engineers for years have attempted to duplicate the human hand, particularly in trying to make prosthetics for people who have lost their hands to injury or disease. While much progress has been made, machines still can't quite work in the same way and with the same efficiency as real hands. Our hands work unlike anything else in creation, which shows God's special touch in the design of human features.

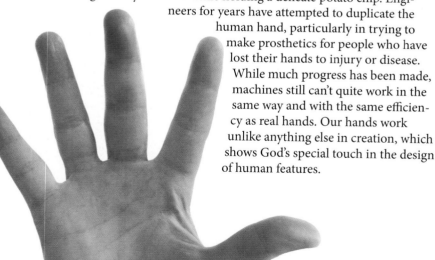

BEES AND BETTER AIRCRAFT

Bees never crash, even when they land on an upside-down surface. Researchers have found that bees have a three-phase landing strategy. A bee first slows to a dead stop and hovers almost exactly 16 millimeters from the surface it is landing on. Second, the bee estimates the slope of the surface, even though it is not moving. Finally, the bee grasps the surface with the appendages nearest to it—with hind feet if it is horizontal or with forefeet if it is inverted, like a ceiling. The bee's landing procedures must be precise because surfaces such as soft flower petals can be shaky. The findings could help engineers make gentler landings for aircraft.

FISH SCALES AND BODY ARMOR

Polypterus senegalus is a type of African freshwater fish that has diamond-shaped "ganoid" scales, each of which is comprised of a series of layers, like in a sandwich. The basement layer is a thin platy bone, and on top of that lies spongy bone, then cosmine (a hard mineral that is like dentine in teeth), and then shiny ganoin enamel that is secreted by the outer skin. Studies showed that not only does each layer offer a unique contribution to the overall strength of the scale, but that the layers are micro-stitched to one another to keep them from peeling apart. Researchers have examined the bony scales of *Polypterus* in an effort to design stronger and lighter body armor.

THE HUMAN BRAIN AND FASTER COMPUTERS

Researchers are studying the human brain in an effort to build faster computers. In today's computers, memory devices are separate from processors, so the two are connected by a channel called a "bus." The size of the bus often determines the flow rate of information, and this can impact the computer's processing capabilities. But processing and memory in our brains, as far as researchers know, operate in the same place and time. This increased efficiency in internal connections has the side benefit of requiring much less energy. The brain consists of billions of neurons that connect with each other via trillions of synapses. Each neuron has vast numbers of individual proteins that act as computational switches, making the total computational power of the human brain literally astronomical. In fact, one recent study compared the number of brain synapses to the number of stars in 1,500 Milky Way galaxies, which could be more than 450 trillion. Just one human brain is far more complex and designed much better than all the computers in the world combined.

GECKO EYES AND NIGHT VISION

Certain gecko lizards can see color in dim light. That means these geckos' eyes are about 350 times more sensitive than human eyes, which see only black and white in the same conditions. In addition to seeing color in the dark, the geckos have built-in correctional abilities for blurred images caused by longitudinal chromatic aberration, or the failure to focus all colors to the same point. Studying these features in gecko eyes may offer clues to improving night-vision camera technology.

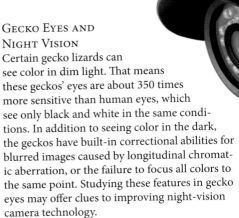

Dinosaurs in Scripture

The book of Genesis uses the word "cattle" to refer to domesticated animals, while "creeping things" refers to small creatures and "beasts of the earth" include the non-domesticated animals. There may have been about 50 or 60 different basic "kinds" of dinosaurs, and their fossils show that they had well-proportioned bodies that were well-designed for the life each led.

In the book of Job, God says, "Look now at the behemoth, which I made along with you; he eats grass like an ox. See now, his strength is in his hips, and his power is in his stomach muscles. He moves his tail like a cedar; the sinews of his thighs are tightly knit. His bones are like beams of bronze, his ribs like bars of iron. He is the first of the ways of God; only He who made him can bring near His sword" (Job 40:15-19). The creature God was describing was most likely what we know as a dinosaur.

Hippopotamus

African elephant

Sauropod

BEHEMOTH

In God's discourse with the prophet Job, He describes how the behemoth "moves his tail like a cedar" (Job 40:15-17). Many Bible commentators inexplicably suggest the creature described here is a hippopotamus or elephant. But neither of those have a tail like a cedar tree. Behemoth had a "tail like a cedar" and lived in a "covert of reeds and marsh" (Job 40:21). As "the first of the ways of God" (Job 40:19), it was very large. The Bible's description of the behemoth best fits a sauropod dinosaur, such as the one illustrated here.

(Left to right) *Compsognathus, Ornitholestes, Dilophosaurus, Torosaurus, Giganotosaurus,* and *Camarasaurus.*

Lebanon Cedar

Corythosaurus

BEASTS OF THE EARTH

Some dinosaurs, like *Compsognathus* or *Mussaurus*, were small "creeping things." But others, like *Tyrannosaurus* or *Ultrasaurus*, were large "beasts of the earth" made alongside man on Day Six of the creation week. Genesis 1:25 states, "And God made the beast of the earth according to its own kind, cattle according to its kind, and everything that creeps on the earth according to its kind." According to Genesis and Job, dinosaurs and man lived at the same time.

ORIGIN OF THE WORD "DINOSAUR"

The King James Bible does not contain the word "dinosaur" because the word did not exist until much later. Dinosaurs were rediscovered (Adam and his progeny saw living dinosaurs first) as fossils in 1822, and the word "dinosaur" was coined in 1841 by biologist and paleontologist Sir Richard Owen—the first superintendent of the prestigious British Museum (Natural History) in London.

Allosaurus

Triceratops

Stegosaurus

COULD THE DINOSAURS FIT ON THE ARK?

Most, if not all, dinosaur fossil layers also have fossil water creatures, like fish and clams. This is consistent with the Flood explanation for their fossilization. But two of every kind of land creature, including dinosaurs, went on board the Ark. Although there are hundreds of named dinosaur species, they belong to only around 60 dinosaur kinds. No matter how large some dinosaurs grew, the largest dinosaur egg was no bigger than a football. Even the *Argentinosaurus*, which could grow up to 120 feet long, would have been represented on the Ark by much smaller and younger specimens. In addition, many dinosaurs were small even when fully grown. The *Sinosauropteryx*—probably of the same kind as *Compsognathus*—was about as big as a turkey. The median size of adult dinosaurs based on fossils was about the size of an American bison, but the average size of juvenile dinosaurs on the Ark was probably closer to that of a sheep. And 120 or so "sheep" would require barely a corner of one of the Ark's three decks.

DINOSAURS AFTER THE FLOOD

We can infer from the reliable Genesis record that after dinosaurs got off the Ark with the other animals, their descendants travelled from the Middle East to places around the globe. This only makes sense, however, when considering that the post-Flood climate was very different from today's climate. During the Ice Age, the Middle East was tropical and regularly watered by heavy rains. This would have set up suitable conditions for dinosaurs to reproduce and fill many Earth environments. Many clues, like dinosaur fossils buried alongside tropical plant fossils and dragon depictions in legends, indicate that dinosaurs lived in swamp-like habitats.

Ceratosaurus

Dinosaurs and Dragon Legends

After the Flood ended about 4,300 years ago, dinosaurs and other animals migrated throughout Europe, China, and the rest of world. After God compelled humans to disperse across the world from Babel, some families migrated into far-flung places where they most likely encountered dinosaurs that had already lived there for hundreds of years. Those encounters have been memorialized in writings, depictions, and legends from people groups across the globe.

Ancient historians described dragons as real, living creatures, right alongside descriptions of other more familiar creatures. Dinosaur depictions occur in carvings, sculptures, bas reliefs, paintings, mosaics, tapestries, sculptures, pictographs, and petroglyphs from all over the world. Some of the telling features that help identify these images as dinosaurian are horns, spiky skin flaps along the spine called dermal frills, long tails, long necks, large teeth, and perhaps most important, legs that went straight down from the body. Those walking reptiles with which we are most familiar today have legs that aim away from the sides of the body, then angle down to the ground at the elbows or knees. Dinosaur reptiles' legs were positioned beneath their bodies (after the likeness of a dog), just as shown on dozens of genuine, ancient depictions.

The vast number of dragon descriptions, and the similarities of those descriptions across geographic space and historical time, are best explained by genuine dinosaur encounters. Many different cultures have similar dragon legends that they could not get from just viewing dinosaur fossils.

ISHTAR GATE

The Babylonian king Nebuchadnezzar II ordered the construction of the Ishtar Gate around 575 B.C. Dedicated to the Babylonian goddess Ishtar, it was the eighth gate that led into the inner parts of the city. The gate featured alternating rows with images of aurochs and dragons, which look nothing like crocodiles. The people of ancient Babylon evidently witnessed these creatures with their own eyes, since they depicted them on the gate with the same level of detail that they did with the easily recognizable aurochs. This image comes from a reconstruction of the gate at the Pergamon Museum in Berlin, Germany.

STEGOSAURUS CARVING ON CAMBODIAN TEMPLE WALL

Ta Prohm is a temple in Angkor, a region in Cambodia. It was built around the late 12th to early 13th centuries to be a monastery and university. Carvings adorn the walls and doorposts of the temple, and one carving features a creature that is clearly a *Stegosaurus*. It appears among other animals that live today, so it makes sense that the artists who made the carvings really saw dinosaurs in their lifetimes.

One of the more fascinating fossil discoveries is the fossilized skull of a creature called *Dracorex hogwartsia*, the first of which was unearthed in South Dakota's Hell Creek Formation. It had spiky horns and a long muzzle, and it was named in honor of the famous *Harry Potter* books by author J. K. Rowling.

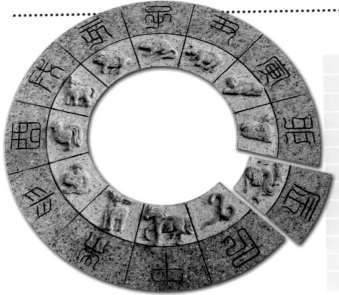

Name	Description	Location or Language
Aziwugum	Giant reptile	Innuit
Bax'an	Terrible water monster	Dakota Sioux
Behemoth	Giant swamp reptile	Hebrew (Job)
Drakon	Dragon	Greece
Grendel	Swamp monster	Denmark
Knucker	Swamp dragon	Wales
Long	Dragon	China
P'ih mw	Giant reptile	Egyptian hieroglyphs
Ro-qua-ho	Giant reptile	Iroquois
Smok	Dragon	Poland
Uk'tena	Horned water monster	Cherokee
Worm (voorm)	Dragon	Germany

CHINESE ZODIAC

The Chinese Zodiac is a system that follows a 12-year cycle that relates each year to an animal and its supposed characteristics. The dragon is supposedly the only mythological creature of the 12 animals featured on the zodiac. Why would nations that have used the zodiac for millennia pick 11 "real" animals and one fictional creature? It is reasonable to think that the ancient East Asians who developed the zodiac really witnessed each of these animals, including the dragon, which could have been a dinosaur.

The word "dragon" can mean one of the many kinds of post-Flood dinosaurs or even flying reptiles. Other languages still use words like those shown in this table.

Petroglyph of what looks like a sauropod at Kachina Bridge in Natural Bridges National Monument, Utah.

ST. GEORGE AND THE DRAGON

St. George was a Greek who served as an officer in the Roman army during the third century A.D. and who is reputed to have fought and slain a dragon. Much debate surrounds the story's origins and veracity. In its most developed form, a dragon set up its nest near a spring, and residents of a nearby city offered a sheep to distract the dragon each time they needed water. But when the sheep ran out, lots were cast for maidens instead. When the lot fell to the princess one day, she was offered to the dragon, but St. George happened by, slew the dragon, and rescued the princess. Historians have drawn parallels between St. George and the Perseus and Andromeda Greek myth, as well as Christianity's opposition to the pagan practices of human sacrifice. Despite the questions surrounding the legend, the fact that it echoes so many similar legends from around the world lends it credibility.

MYTHS AND FALLACIES

*"Guard what was committed
to your trust, avoiding the
profane and idle babblings
and contradictions of what is
falsely called knowledge."
(1 Timothy 6:20)*

Charles Darwin

Charles Robert Darwin (1809-1882) was a British naturalist who is famous for popularizing the hypothesis that all living things descended over vast ages from common ancestors. He published his theory of evolution by natural selection in 1859 as a book titled *On the Origin of Species*. Many secularists accept Darwin's theory as the unifying theory of the life sciences and the explanation for the diversity we see in all living creatures.

This marble statue of Charles Darwin was sculpted by Sir Joseph Boehm in 1885. It is housed in the Natural History Museum in London.

However, Darwin's theory is not a scientific one, based on the definition of what a scientific theory is. Scientific theories are repeatedly confirmed through observation and experimentation. While researchers observe variations within an animal kind (e.g., zebras, horses, and donkeys are from the same kind because they can successfully interbreed), we have never observed a species turning into another species. The fossil record contains no undisputed "missing links." In fact, for every proposed transitional form, there is at least one evolutionist who has refuted it on scientific grounds.

VOYAGE WITH THE *HMS BEAGLE*

After Darwin dropped out of medical school to study theology, he started studying nature and began collecting different species of beetles. Upon graduation, he was invited to board the *HMS Beagle* on an expedition to South America. Darwin made several important observations during the trip, but he was heavily influenced by Charles Lyell's idea of geologic uniformitarianism and old Earth ages. With this bias, Darwin drew several mistaken conclusions from his observations that led to the formation of his theory of evolution.

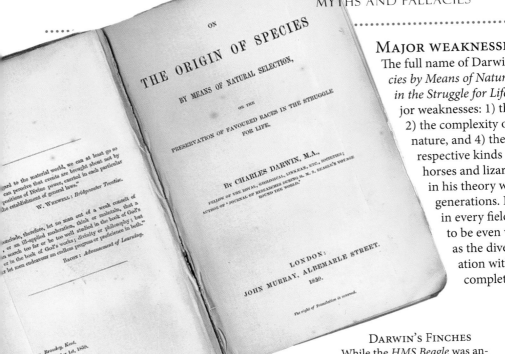

MAJOR WEAKNESSES IN *ON THE ORIGIN OF SPECIES*

The full name of Darwin's famous 1859 treatise is *On the Origin of Species by Means of Natural Selection, or the Preservation of Favoured Races in the Struggle for Life*. Darwin admitted that his theory had four major weaknesses: 1) the lack of transitional forms in the fossil record, 2) the complexity of organs, 3) the stunning instincts of creatures in nature, and 4) the inability for creatures to breed outside of their respective kinds (e.g., horses and donkeys can interbreed, but horses and lizards cannot). Darwin had hoped that these flaws in his theory would be solved by the scientific research of future generations. However, as more and more discoveries are made in every field of scientific inquiry, Darwin's theory has proved to be even weaker. And even his evidences of evolution, such as the diversity of finch beak shapes and sizes, show variation within a particular animal kind, *not* evolution into completely new animal types.

DARWIN'S FINCHES

While the *HMS Beagle* was anchored in the Galapagos Islands, Darwin studied a number of different animals, especially the numerous varieties of finches. He particularly was interested in their different beak sizes and shapes. He interpreted the differences to mean that the finches' beaks evolved after they migrated to the islands and that environmental pressures caused the changes. However, researchers later observed finch beaks "de-evolving," or changing back after a few generations, which goes against Darwin's theory. Despite the changes in their beaks, the finches are still finches, and they have not turned into any other kind of animal.

1. Geospiza magnirostris.
2. Geospiza fortis.
3. Geospiza parvula.
4. Certhidea olivaㅣea.

DARWIN'S "TREE OF LIFE"

In 1837, Darwin drew his first "evolutionary tree" in one of his notebooks with the words "I think" scrawled above it. The tree was to illustrate his idea that all of today's species arose from a single common ancestor. Since then, several different evolutionary trees have been developed by evolutionists over the years to try to explain living things, but none of them fit what we see. Especially with ongoing research in fields that didn't exist in Darwin's day, such as genetics, we are learning that every creature is uniquely designed.

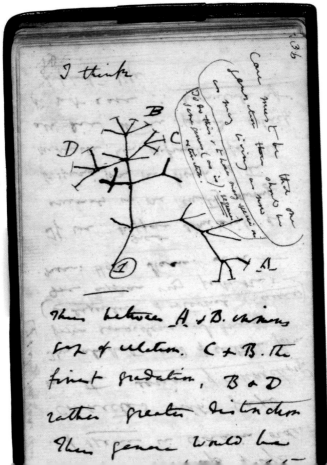

ALFRED RUSSEL WALLACE

Another British naturalist named Alfred Russel Wallace independently formed his own theory of evolution through natural selection, though he did not use the same terms as Darwin. He once briefly met and then corresponded with Darwin, and even sent him an essay called *On the Tendency of Varieties to Depart Indefinitely From the Original Type* for review. Darwin passed Wallace's essay on to his friends Charles Lyell and botanist Joseph Hooker, who decided to publish the paper for Wallace in 1858. Unlike Darwin, Wallace traveled extensively for his research, and he already believed in the transmutation of species. Darwin didn't believe that until after his voyage aboard the *Beagle*.

Transitional Forms Don't Exist

Transitional forms are what evolutionary scientists hope to find in nature to help bolster Charles Darwin's theory of evolution through natural selection. Darwin, at the time of publishing *On the Origin of Species*, noted the lack of transitional fossils in existence, and he hoped that they would be found by future generations of researchers. Several fossils have been heralded as "missing links" by academia and popular media over the years, only to then be quietly refuted or found to be hoaxes after more in-depth analysis. In short, no transitional forms have been found, either in the fossil record or among present living creatures.

DID YOU KNOW?

Evolution necessarily implies the concept of "descent from a common ancestor or ancestors." Yet no ancestor/descendant relationship can be advocated with certainty based on the fossil record. In fact, for every proposed transitional form, there is at least one evolutionary scientist who has refuted it on scientific grounds.

ARCHAEOPTERYX

Archaeopteryx is a supposed link via therapod dinosaurs between reptiles and birds. Upon closer inspection, this fossil is found to have been fully bird and not transitional at all. Unlike dinosaurs, *Archaeopteryx* had a large braincase for the increased motor control and sensory input required for flight. It also had a robust furcula (wishbone) that kept its flight muscles from crushing the bird's delicate internal air sacs. No evidence supports the story that such fully formed wings with fused clavicles "evolved from" the tiny, clavicle-free theropod forelimbs. Even claw measurements of *Archaeopteryx* fall within the range of true perching birds. It was a bird without a single transitional feature.

TIKTAALIK

Some secular researchers discovered and labeled the extinct fish *Tiktaalik* as a transitional form in 2003. It had an amphibian-like flat head with its eyes on top. Its neck was also unattached to its shoulder bone, allowing it to freely rotate its head more like an amphibian than a fish. However, it had gills, scales, and fins, which are dominant fish traits. It also lived in the water, and its body structure, such as its weak backbone in the pelvic region, meant that it was suited for swimming and not walking. *Tiktaalik* was completely a fish and not a transitional form at all.

FEATHERED DINOSAURS?

Most museums and textbooks that have dinosaur displays or pictures also include artistic renderings of dinosaurs sporting colorful feathers. These depictions seem to support the recently popular doctrine that an as-yet-unidentified theropod dinosaur evolved into the first bird, which then evolved into all other bird kinds. But not all evolutionary researchers agree that fossil dinosaurs had feathers. And dinosaur skin was covered in scales, closer to reptiles than birds. Overall, there are far more reasons to doubt the feathered dinosaur idea than there are reasons to affirm it.

Dinosaur fossils have been found with "fibers," which some scientists interpret to be the beginnings of feathers. However, upon closer analysis, the fibers don't have the same structure as feathers, and they were later called "filaments" as part of the skin structure. In short, they were not feathers, nor the beginnings of feathers. Also, neither dinosaur skin impressions nor original dinosaur skin has large follicles like those that produce feathers in bird skin. And actual bird fossils are found mixed in among dinosaur remains (something that museums and textbooks often don't show). Ducks, loons, albatross, other water birds and parrots, as well as extinct bird kinds, had clawed wings. How could dinosaurs evolve pre-feathers if real feathers were already on the scene? And what purpose would bird feathers serve on those tough dinosaur hides? Feathered dinosaurs simply do not fit the fossil evidence.

Even if dinosaurs were found with feathers, the rest of their anatomy is so different from birds that they could not possibly have evolved into them, even given millions of years. Theropod dinosaurs have exactly the wrong body structure for flight. A bird's center of gravity is balanced between its wings in the front of its body, and a dinosaur's center of gravity is balanced over its thighs near the back of its body. Transmutating a dinosaur skeleton into a bird skeleton would have rendered the transitional creatures unfit, being unable to either fly or walk properly. One study demonstrated that if a bird's legs or ribs were removed or significantly altered, the resulting creature would suffocate. They would've been extinct before they had a chance to evolve.

Fossil dinosaur skin does not have the follicles that produce feathers. Instead, it consists of tightly arranged reptilian scales.

Evolutionists consider *Homo habilis* to be a species in the same genus (*Homo*) as humans. But *H. habilis* had long curved fingers and long curved toes. Creatures with such anatomical features use them only for swinging from tree branch to tree branch, not for walking upright like humans. In short, *H. habilis* is an extinct variety of the ape kind and not a transitional form.

Humans vs. Apes

We are often taught in school that humans and apes shared a common evolutionary ancestor. However, this is not what Scripture says, and the scientific evidence doesn't support that idea either. The first chapter of the book of Genesis clearly states that humans were made by God in His image to be distinct from the rest of creation. A closer look at the scarce human and ape fossils that have been found, as well as the molecular evidence, shows that humans and apes are very distinct creations with no common shared "ancestry."

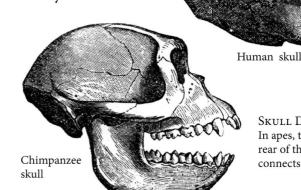

Human skull

Chimpanzee skull

SKULL DIFFERENCES
In apes, the spine connects to the rear of the skull. But the human spine connects to the bottom of the skull.

The human spine is designed differently from those of other creatures. When God made humans in His image, He engineered the "S" curve in our backs perfectly to hold our heads upright and efficiently transfer our body weight to our hips. That works with our other body structures so we can stand and move on two feet. No other body design in creation is like the human design, showing that God made us to be unique.

99% GENETICALLY SIMILAR?
Evolutionary researchers like to say that humans and chimpanzees are 99 percent genetically similar. What they don't tend to say is that this number comes from very unscientific methods. Out of the human and genetic information currently available to us, some researchers have chosen to study a very, very small portion of the genomes—specifically, the portions that are most similar. When the entire sequence is compared, humans and chimpanzees are really only about 84 percent similar. Genetic information shows that humans and apes are very different, and any similarities point more to a similar Creator than a similar ancestor.

LUCY

In 1974, a partially complete skeleton was discovered in Ethiopia by American paleoanthropologist Donald Johanson. The skeleton was classified under the genus *Australopithecus* and named "Lucy" after the Beatles' song "Lucy in the Sky with Diamonds." It was estimated to be about 3.2 million years old and stood about 3.5 feet tall. Certain features suggested to Johanson that it may have walked erect and was therefore evolving into a human. However, Lucy is only a 40 percent complete skeleton, and the bones that it does have show that it was more like an ape and nothing like a human. Since its discovery, closer analysis of Lucy's skeleton has raised so many questions among both secular and creation scientists that it has since been quietly deemed not a human evolutionary ancestor. It was most likely an extinct ape. However, some textbooks and museum displays still tout it as an evolutionary ancestor to humans without presenting any of the real data.

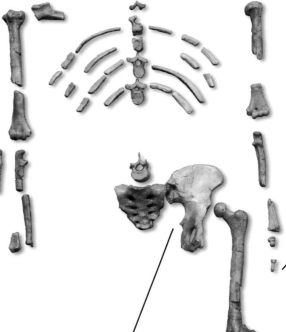

A complete skull wasn't recovered for Lucy, but other australopithecine fossil skulls are shaped more like ape skulls than human skulls.

Finger bones recovered with Lucy's partially complete skeleton, as well as from other *Australopithecus* fossils, are long and curved, more like apes than humans. That's because they were made to be able to climb and swing from trees. While apes have been observed to mimic human behavior and use tools to get food, ape hands still lack the ability to do a lot of the things human hands can do.

OTHER "MISSING LINKS"

Other fossils that have been heralded as human evolutionary ancestors since the hype over the Lucy skeleton include "Ardi" and "Ida" (*Darwinius masillae*, pictured here). Ardi's (*Ardipithecus ramidus*) fossilized remains were first found along the Awash River in Ethiopia, and Ida's fossil was found in Germany. Ardi was later found to be just an extinct ape and Ida was an extinct lemur-like creature, neither of which have any human-like or transitional features.

A complete pelvis wasn't recovered with the rest of Lucy's bones, and that's important for determining whether or not the creature was able to walk upright.

Australopithecines like Lucy may have been able walk somewhat upright, as pygmy chimps do today, but not in the human manner at all. Johanson's claim for Lucy's ability to walk upright (despite not having found the skeleton's pelvis) came from finding a knee joint located two or three kilometers away in a layer of rock about 200 feet lower than where he found Lucy. Clearly, the knee does not belong with the rest. But even if they do go together, the knee is not diagnostically upright, and that points more specifically to tree-climbing abilities.

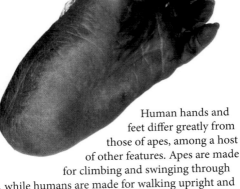

Human hands and feet differ greatly from those of apes, among a host of other features. Apes are made for climbing and swinging through trees, while humans are made for walking upright and working with our hands. Our spines are also ideally designed for walking and standing on two feet, which differs greatly from the structure of ape spines.

Bad Design?

Evolutionists like to argue that all sorts of anatomical parts are poorly designed, and that they supposedly could not be designed by an infinitely wise deity. However, they generally are ignorant of the full function of the parts they criticize, as well as the principles governing design. In reality, creatures in their prime normally do exhibit breathtaking fit and finish, and claims that something is poorly designed are not equivalent to data-supported facts.

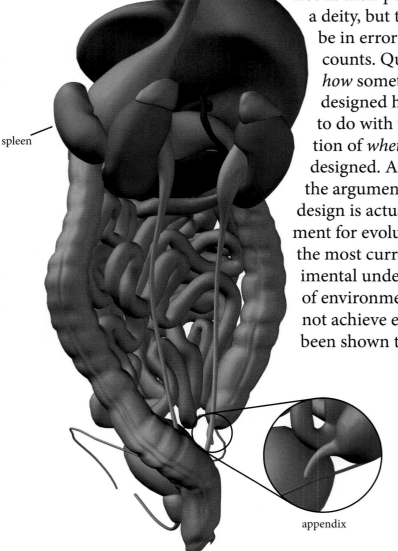

spleen

appendix

"Bad design" claims are generally not scientific, but theological. The claimants' perception of a design does not fit their perception of a deity, but they could be in error on both counts. Questioning *how* something was designed has nothing to do with the question of *whether* it was designed. And none of the arguments against design is actually an argument for evolution. From the most current experimental understanding of environments, environmental processes alone do not achieve even shoddy design. In fact, they have not been shown to produce *any* design.

Multiple Functions

"Bad design" arguments may be overlooking, from a design perspective, the need to balance several competing interests (e.g., obtaining an optimized design). The knife on a multi-tool is not ideal for use in the kitchen of a five-star restaurant, but it is not a bad design. Just because a design does not maximize the performance of one particular trait doesn't mean the whole entity was not designed. There may be good reasons for design tradeoffs between various traits, and others have probably not been discovered yet. Design tradeoffs are actually a better indicator of intelligence behind a design.

The spleen acts as a blood filter. While we do not need it to survive, if there's nothing wrong with it, it is best to keep it in place and let it do what it was made to do.

Studies have shown that the vermiform appendix (simply known as the appendix) is part of an optimally functioning immune system.

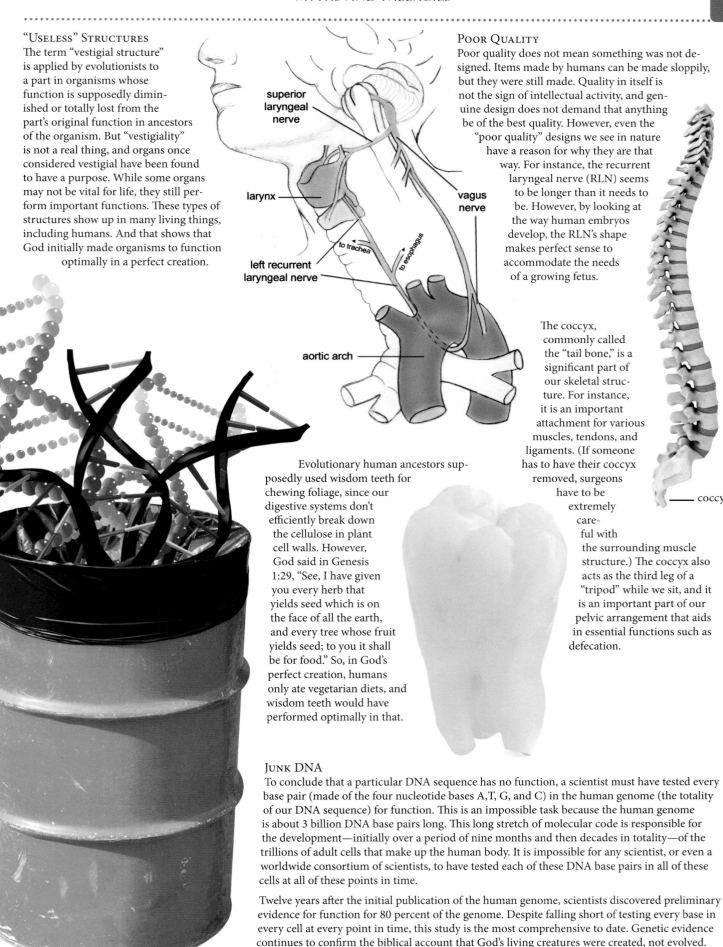

"USELESS" STRUCTURES

The term "vestigial structure" is applied by evolutionists to a part in organisms whose function is supposedly diminished or totally lost from the part's original function in ancestors of the organism. But "vestigiality" is not a real thing, and organs once considered vestigial have been found to have a purpose. While some organs may not be vital for life, they still perform important functions. These types of structures show up in many living things, including humans. And that shows that God initially made organisms to function optimally in a perfect creation.

superior
laryngeal
nerve

larynx

left recurrent
laryngeal nerve

to trachea

to esophagus

vagus
nerve

aortic arch

POOR QUALITY

Poor quality does not mean something was not designed. Items made by humans can be made sloppily, but they were still made. Quality in itself is not the sign of intellectual activity, and genuine design does not demand that anything be of the best quality. However, even the "poor quality" designs we see in nature have a reason for why they are that way. For instance, the recurrent laryngeal nerve (RLN) seems to be longer than it needs to be. However, by looking at the way human embryos develop, the RLN's shape makes perfect sense to accommodate the needs of a growing fetus.

The coccyx, commonly called the "tail bone," is a significant part of our skeletal structure. For instance, it is an important attachment for various muscles, tendons, and ligaments. (If someone has to have their coccyx removed, surgeons have to be extremely careful with the surrounding muscle structure.) The coccyx also acts as the third leg of a "tripod" while we sit, and it is an important part of our pelvic arrangement that aids in essential functions such as defecation.

coccyx

Evolutionary human ancestors supposedly used wisdom teeth for chewing foliage, since our digestive systems don't efficiently break down the cellulose in plant cell walls. However, God said in Genesis 1:29, "See, I have given you every herb that yields seed which is on the face of all the earth, and every tree whose fruit yields seed; to you it shall be for food." So, in God's perfect creation, humans only ate vegetarian diets, and wisdom teeth would have performed optimally in that.

JUNK DNA

To conclude that a particular DNA sequence has no function, a scientist must have tested every base pair (made of the four nucleotide bases A, T, G, and C) in the human genome (the totality of our DNA sequence) for function. This is an impossible task because the human genome is about 3 billion DNA base pairs long. This long stretch of molecular code is responsible for the development—initially over a period of nine months and then decades in totality—of the trillions of adult cells that make up the human body. It is impossible for any scientist, or even a worldwide consortium of scientists, to have tested each of these DNA base pairs in all of these cells at all of these points in time.

Twelve years after the initial publication of the human genome, scientists discovered preliminary evidence for function for 80 percent of the genome. Despite falling short of testing every base in every cell at every point in time, this study is the most comprehensive to date. Genetic evidence continues to confirm the biblical account that God's living creatures were created, not evolved.

Naturalistic Attempts Fail to Explain Life Origins

Wanting to understand our origins is a part of human nature. But the fact is that any attempt to understand who we are, why we're here, and where we came from fails without Scripture. While science allows us to study the chemical compounds that living things contain and use, it cannot show us how to use those chemicals to make life occur. Life is far more complex than the specific arrangement of the chemical compounds needed to support life—which can never self-assemble through random natural processes. Life and its origins can only make sense in terms of a living, powerful, and creative God who arranged just the right materials in the right order, proportions, conditions, and time with the appropriate information for a living organism to maintain itself and reproduce.

Ernst Haeckel

Ernst Heinrich Philipp August Haeckel (1834-1919) was a German biologist and artist who promoted Charles Darwin's work in Germany, including Darwin's idea of an "evolutionary tree of life" (also known as phylogenetic trees). Haeckel also developed his own tree in an attempt to show the evolution of all living things, including humans. Just like other phylogenetic trees drawn over the years, it contains errors and inconsistencies but still tends to appear in modern science textbooks. Study after study has revealed even more problems with evolutionary lineages derived from molecular data than with lineages derived from morphological data. Furthermore, lineages based upon biological sequence data often contradict lineages based upon morphological data. The fact that it has been impossible to objectively establish evolutionary relationships between so many creatures reflects an underlying reality—evolution never occurred.

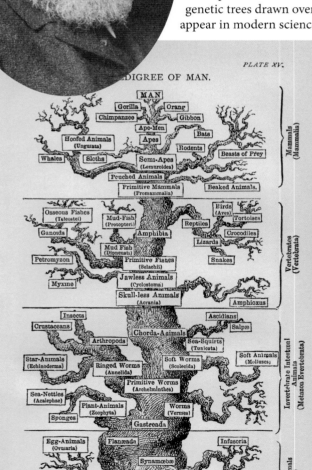

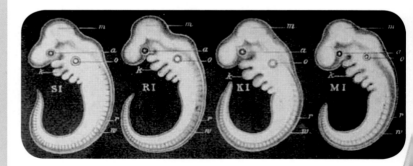

Embryological Drawings

Haeckel was very interested in embryology as a student, and in 1868 he made a series of illustrations that supposedly show the stages of a human embryo's development. The idea was that human embryos look like animal embryos (such as dog, turtle, and hen) during different stages of development. He presented these drawings as definitive proof of evolution. Since the advent of modern technology, we know that human embryos are unique from animal embryos at all developmental stages, and yet Haeckel's drawings still appear in modern biology and even medical textbooks.

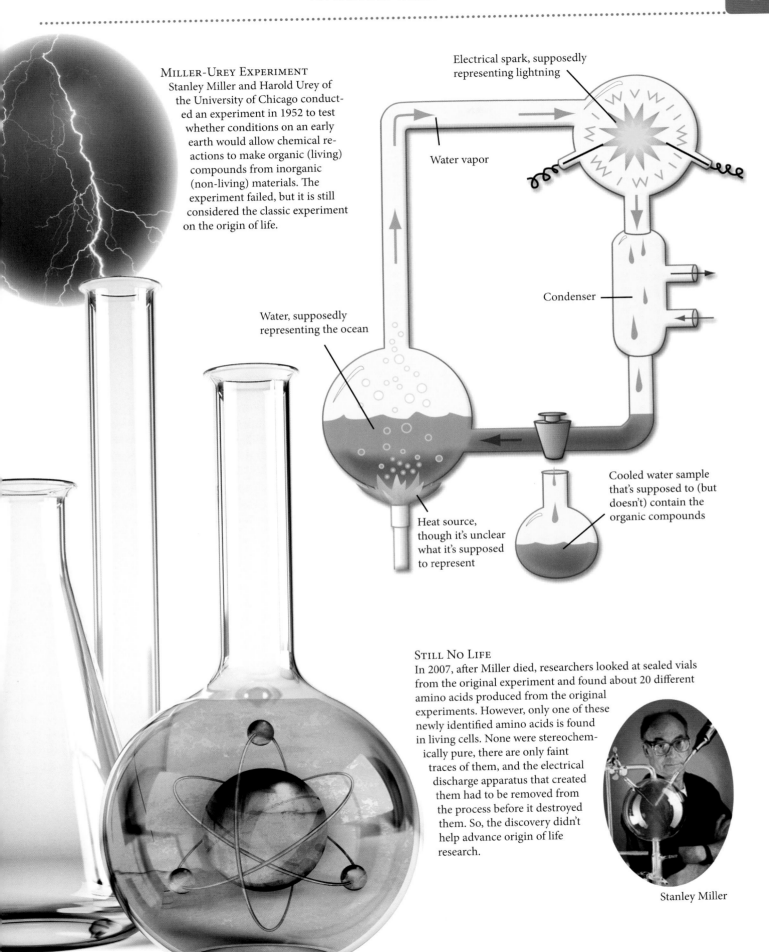

MILLER-UREY EXPERIMENT
Stanley Miller and Harold Urey of the University of Chicago conducted an experiment in 1952 to test whether conditions on an early earth would allow chemical reactions to make organic (living) compounds from inorganic (non-living) materials. The experiment failed, but it is still considered the classic experiment on the origin of life.

Electrical spark, supposedly representing lightning

Water vapor

Condenser

Water, supposedly representing the ocean

Heat source, though it's unclear what it's supposed to represent

Cooled water sample that's supposed to (but doesn't) contain the organic compounds

STILL NO LIFE
In 2007, after Miller died, researchers looked at sealed vials from the original experiment and found about 20 different amino acids produced from the original experiments. However, only one of these newly identified amino acids is found in living cells. None were stereochemically pure, there are only faint traces of them, and the electrical discharge apparatus that created them had to be removed from the process before it destroyed them. So, the discovery didn't help advance origin of life research.

Stanley Miller

Compromises to the Genesis Timeline

Some try to compromise the teaching that Earth is billions of years old with Scripture. This doesn't work, however, because Scripture is clear on Earth's origins and history. The six-day recent creation is affirmed throughout the Bible and lays the foundation for everything that has happened since, including our need for the salvation that only comes through Jesus' life, death, and resurrection. We can have complete confidence in the authority of God's Word because Scripture is straightforward and accurate in its recording of historical events, and both scriptural and scientific evidence support the Genesis creation account.

DEFINITION OF A DAY

On Day One, after creating the heavens and the earth, God created light and "divided the light from the darkness" (Genesis 1:4). This light/dark cycle was further identified when "God called the light Day [Hebrew *yom*], and the darkness He called Night" (Genesis 1:5). Throughout the rest of the passage, He uses the same term for the first day through the seventh day. The meaning of the term "day" is further limited by the use of the modifying terms "evening" and "morning." The Old Testament uses this combination 38 times, and each time means a normal day. Furthermore, Exodus 20:11 states, "For in six days the LORD made the heavens and the earth, the sea, and all that is in them, and rested the seventh day." The same word *yom* is used here in the same context as the *yom* used for the days of the creation week.

Timeframe "Links"	Bookend Events	Womb Time	Stated Years	Partial Year	Total Years
1. Genesis 5:3	Adam is created / Adam begets Seth	n/a	130	≤ 1	≤ 131
2. Genesis 5:6	Seth is begotten / Seth begets Enosh	≤ 1	105	≤ 1	≤ 107
3. Genesis 5:9	Enosh is begotten / Enosh begets Cainan	≤ 1	90	≤ 1	≤ 92
4. Genesis 5:12	Cainan is begotten / C. begets Mahalaleel	≤ 1	70	≤ 1	≤ 72
5. Genesis 5:15	Mahalaleel is begotten / M. begets Jared	≤ 1	65	≤ 1	≤ 67
6. Genesis 5:18	Jared is begotten / Jared begts Enoch	≤ 1	162	≤ 1	≤ 164
7. Genesis 5:21	Enoch is begotten / E. begets Methuselah	≤ 1	65	≤ 1	≤ 67
8. Genesis 5:25	Methuselah is begotten / M. begets Lamech	≤ 1	187	≤ 1	≤ 189
9. Genesis 5:28-29	Lamech is begotten / Lamech begets Noah	≤ 1	182	≤ 1	≤ 184
10. Genesis 7:6	Noah is begotten / Flood hits	≤ 1	600	≤ 1	≤ 602
11. Genesis 11:10	Flood hits / Arphaxad is begotten	n/a	2	≤ 1	≤ 3
12. Genesis 11:12	Arphaxad is begotten / A. begets Shelah	≤ 1	35	≤ 1	≤ 37
13. Genesis 11:14	Shelah is begotten / Shelah begets Eber	≤ 1	30	≤ 1	≤ 32
14. Genesis 11:16	Eber is begotten / Eber begets Peleg	≤ 1	34	≤ 1	≤ 36
15. Genesis 11:18	Peleg is begotten / Peleg begets Reu	≤ 1	30	≤ 1	≤ 32
16. Genesis 11:20	Reu is begotten / Reu begets Serug	≤ 1	32	≤ 1	≤ 34
17. Genesis 11:22	Serug is begotten / Serug begets Nahor	≤ 1	30	≤ 1	≤ 32
18. Genesis 11:24	Nahor is begotten / Nahor begets Terah	≤ 1	29	≤ 1	≤ 31
19. Genesis 11:26	Terah is begotten / Abraham is born	≤1=≤1	70	≤ 1	≤ 73
			Total: ≥1,948		Total: ≤1,985

The timeframe in years from Adam's creation to Abraham's birth, based on event-to-event timeframe "links" as recorded in Genesis

TIME SINCE CREATION

Abraham lived around 2000 B.C. (about 4,000 years ago), a date accepted by historians, archaeologists, and biblical students. Before Abraham, the timeframes given in Genesis are measured by the number of years between one event and another event, regardless of how many generations occurred between those "bookend" events. Even taking into account factors such as partial years and the Flood, it is straight event-to-event math to discover the age of the earth.

Using generous qualifications for gestation periods and for birthday-qualified partial years, the qualified timeframe becomes:

Least time: 130 + 105 + 90 + 70 + 65 + 162 + 65 + 187 + 182 + 600 + 2 + 35 + 30 + 34 + 30 + 32 + 30 + 29 + 70 = **not less than 1,948 years**

Most time: 131 + 107 + 92 + 72 + 67 + 164 + 67 + 189 + 184 + 602 + 3 + 37 + 32 + 36 + 32 + 34 + 32 + 31 + 73 = **not more than 1,985 years**

The total earth-time in years from God's creation of Adam to the birth of Abraham cannot be more than 1,985 years—although it is likely somewhat less than that—and it cannot be less than 1,948 years. Include the six days of creation and the one day of rest, and you have the age of the earth being about 6,000 years. When other ancient manuscripts of Scripture are considered, the most extreme case we arrive at is that Earth (and the universe) is about 10,000 years old.

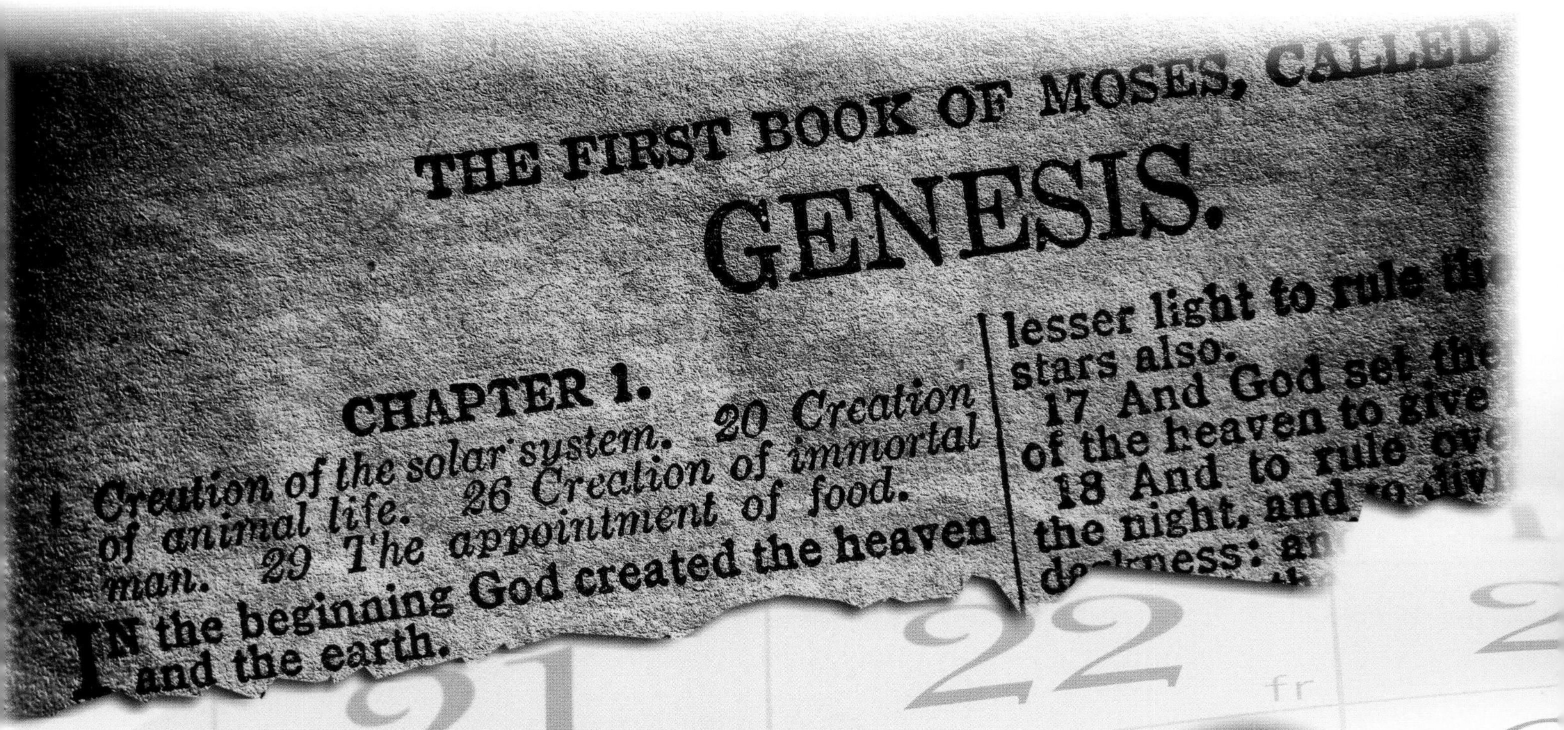

THE FIRST BOOK OF MOSES, CALLED

GENESIS.

CHAPTER 1.

Creation of the solar system. 20 Creation of animal life. 26 Creation of immortal man. 29 The appointment of food.

IN the beginning God created the heaven and the earth.

lesser light to rule th
stars also.
17 And God set th
of the heaven to give
18 And to rule ov
the night, and
darkness:

GAP THEORY AND DAY AGE THEORY

Some have suggested that there was an enormous gap of time between Genesis 1:1 and 1:2, redefining the creation week as more of a "re-creation" (i.e., restoration) week. Supposedly, God originally made the world billions of years ago and then it was ruined, perhaps by Satan, so that the creation week "days" of Genesis 1 recount how He re-made the world in six ordinary days. This view is called "the gap theory," originally proposed by the Scottish theology professor Thomas Chalmers about 45 years before Charles Darwin published *On the Origin of Species*. It was an attempt to "harmonize" biblical history with "old earth" teachings from men such as geologists Charles Lyell (who greatly influenced Darwin) and James Hutton. However, the gap theory doesn't fit what Scripture says at all.

Another attempt from the 19th century to compromise Scripture with old-earth histories is to redefine *yom*, used to describe the days of the creation week, to mean "age." The theory goes that each of the creation "days" could have lasted epochs in cosmic history. But "age" isn't what *yom* means, so this "day age" theory also doesn't fit what Scripture says. In addition, the order of creation is totally different from the "order" of evolution.

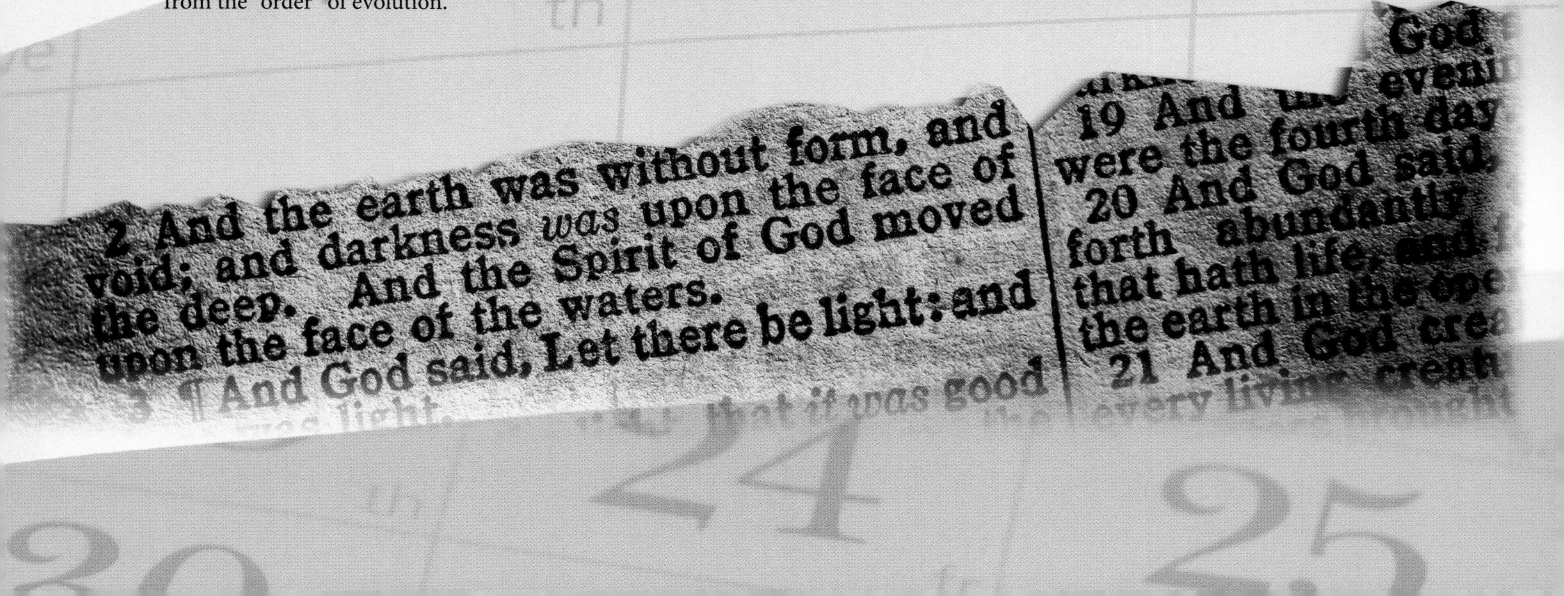

Thomas Chalmers

God
eveni
19 And th
were the fourth day
20 And God said
forth abundantly
that hath life, and
the earth in the ope
21 And God cre

2 And the earth was without form, and void; and darkness *was* upon the face of the deep. And the Spirit of God moved upon the face of the waters.
3 ¶ And God said, Let there be light: and
that it was good

UFO Myths

Are there aliens and UFOs in God's creation? The term UFO stands for "unidentified flying object." So, any flying object that you cannot identify is technically (to you) a UFO. They can be perfectly ordinary objects or phenomena—planes, birds, stars, planets, satellites, meteors, aurorae, lightning, and so on—that some people simply cannot identify.

Due to the strong influence of science fiction and evolutionary stories in our nation, many people associate the term UFO with "aliens." But virtually all reported UFOs are readily explained by natural or man-made items. Even the idea of interstellar travel is far less feasible than the simple "warp-drive" depictions from science fiction would lead people to believe. There are fundamental difficulties that advances in technology cannot simply circumvent.

Scripture seems to strongly imply that Earth is unique among the creation. Earth was made on Day One of the creation week, but all the celestial lights (stars and other planets) were made on Day Four (Genesis 1:16-19). And the Bible states that Earth was specifically designed for life. This is clear in Genesis 1 and is summarized in Isaiah 45:18. The heavens certainly reflect God's glory (Psalm 19:1), and they mark the passage of time (Genesis 1:14), but they are not designed to house life.

The Bible teaches that because of Adam's sin, the universe is cursed (Romans 8:20-23, Genesis 3:17-19). Jesus became a human to offer Himself as a substitute for us, Adam's descendants. Even if "aliens" were real, they wouldn't be related to Christ (i.e., human) and therefore Christ didn't die for them. If they can't be saved, then God would be unjust. But we know that God is just and righteous, and therefore Earth must be the only place God created intelligent life.

METEORS

A meteor—or a "shooting star" or "falling star"—can also be a UFO. A meteor is the bright, very brief trail produced by a piece of dust or a pebble that enters Earth's atmosphere from space. Since the intruder moves at thousands of miles per hour, it is heated by air resistance and is usually quickly vaporized. Sometimes meteors can be very bright, even brighter than the full moon, in which case they are called "fireballs." And sometimes meteors leave a fainter glowing trail, usually light blue in color, that lasts for a few seconds and is called a "train." On rare occasions, the faint train can last for several minutes, in which case it is called a "persistent train."

VENUS

The most commonly reported UFO is the planet Venus, which often appears in the western sky just after sunset or in the morning sky just before sunrise. The planet is brighter than any nighttime star or other planet, and this brightness sometimes surprises some people. Venus can appear to shimmer, twinkle, or rapidly change color when it is very low in the sky. This is due to turbulence in Earth's atmosphere, which causes minor deviations in the path of the incoming light. It may seem strange to those people who see it for the first time, but it's all natural.

OTHER UFOs

There are rare natural phenomena that can also be reported as UFOs. One example is called "ball lightning." This rare and somewhat controversial phenomenon seems to manifest as a spherical, persistent ball of electrical activity associated with storms. Since it is so rare and strange, some would count it as an unidentified flying object.

MAN-MADE SATELLITES

Satellites are sometimes reported as UFOs because they can appear as faint moving "stars." They are easy to see on dark summer nights because the angle of the sun relative to Earth is optimal that time of year. You can easily see a dozen or more satellites on a summer evening if you stay up late for a few hours.

ABDUCTION STORIES

Occasionally, we hear a report of someone who claims to have been actually abducted by aliens. Perhaps some people genuinely do think that they have had some such kind of inexplicable experience. But the fact is that our senses are not always perfectly reliable. Magicians rely upon this fact, and there are conditions that can exacerbate our misperceptions of the world. Alcohol and other substance abuse can cause people to have all sorts of unreal experiences, but there are also medical conditions that, through no fault of the person, can cause severe hallucinations, panic attacks, and so on.

ARE ALIENS DEMONS?

Some Christians have suggested demonic activity as the source for supposed alien experiences. But demons are spirits and do not have physical flesh and cannot manifest physically. God alone has the power to create flesh (John 1:3). On some occasions, God provided temporary bodies for His angels so that they could physically interact with people. But this was by His power, not the angels.' Angels cannot create. It does not make sense that God would make bodies for fallen angels and certainly not for the purpose of tricking people into believing in aliens.

The Bible doesn't tell us much about what angels (godly or fallen) can do in terms of the physical creation. But we know that Satan can tempt, so he does have at least a limited ability to influence people's thoughts. It is feasible that people who have opened themselves up to anti-Christian spiritualism have had demonic experiences in their mind (though not physically). But Christians have nothing to fear, since we enjoy the protection of Almighty God. The Satanic powers of the world fear and flee from us as we submit to God (James 4:7).

"Iridium flares" are often reported as a UFO sighting. They happen when communications satellites produced by the satellite communications company Iridium occasionally catch the sunlight at just the right angle. When this happens, the satellites become extremely bright for several seconds—even outshining Venus! Iridium flares are completely predictable, and some websites can compute when they will happen at given locations.

FOUNDATION
TO
CREATION

*"Then God saw everything
that He had made, and
indeed it was very good."*
(Genesis 1:31)

Genesis

The Bible's book of Genesis tells us how God historically created everything. Accordingly, the Bible reveals what we could never know otherwise about our origins, such as where we came from, how we got here, and why God made us. In Genesis, we learn that the world was once absolutely perfect, the "very good" creation of an infinitely holy and most loving God. People today are descended from Adam and Eve, and have inherited a sin-nature from them. Apart from Genesis, the gospel message makes no sense.

GENESIS IS WRITTEN AS HISTORY

Some make the argument that Genesis is poetic, when in actuality it's written as narrative history. English poetry is defined by its verbal "hardware," with pronounced sounds and rhythms qualifying the text as poetry. Hebrew poetry, however, is defined by its "software," or its verbal information and meaning presented with parallelism of thought (not sound). In short, Hebrew poetry is defined by parallelism in meaning, whereas English poetry is defined by the format of verse and sound (rhyme, alliteration, assonance, and/or meter). The sentences in Genesis read like narrative history, not poetry.

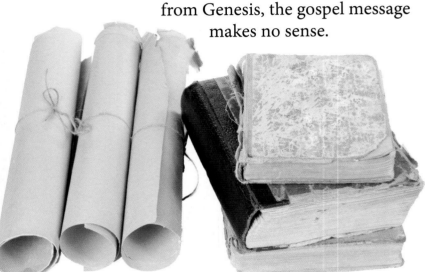

THE FOUNDATION FOR LAWS

Civil laws, moral laws, and so forth all have one thing in common—they put limitations on our behavior by threatening some sort of penalty for noncompliance. The first laws were given to human beings by God in Genesis, when He told Adam not to eat of the tree of the knowledge of good and evil (Genesis 2:17). The reason we have laws is because God made us in His image. He therefore has the right to set rules for our behavior. And since He gave us free will, He attached unpleasant penalties when laws are broken, and He promised blessings for obedience (e.g., Deuteronomy 28:1-14). We owe God our very existence, and so we have a moral obligation to obey any laws He has set forth. Additionally, we have a very good reason to obey God—He will hold us accountable for our actions, and there will be a final judgment. Moreover, since we have a natural proclivity toward evil (inherited from our rebellious ancestor Adam), civil laws are also necessary to restrain evil in society. Laws make sense in light of the history given in Genesis.

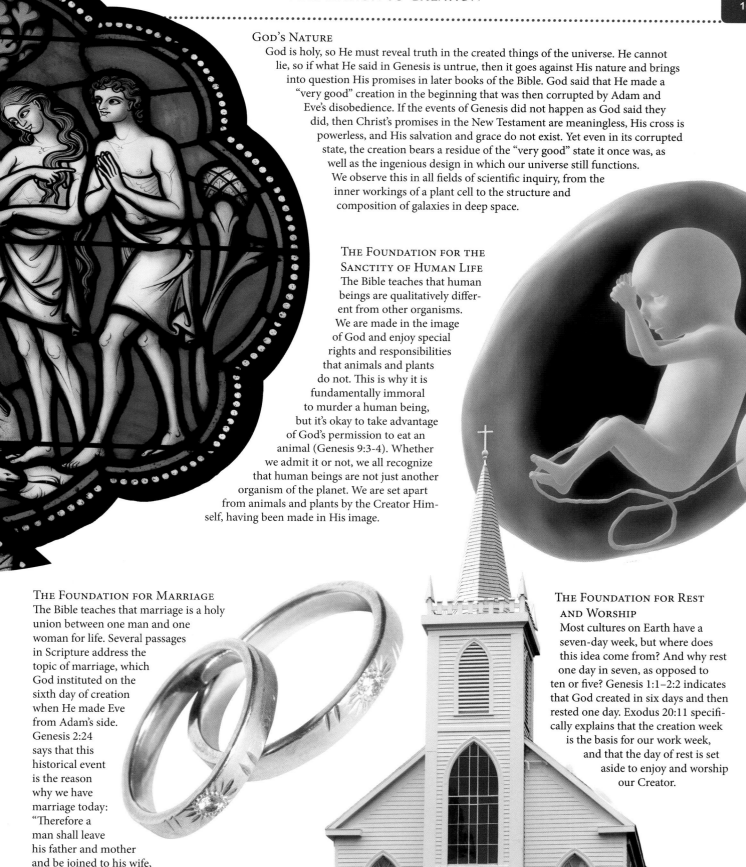

God's Nature

God is holy, so He must reveal truth in the created things of the universe. He cannot lie, so if what He said in Genesis is untrue, then it goes against His nature and brings into question His promises in later books of the Bible. God said that He made a "very good" creation in the beginning that was then corrupted by Adam and Eve's disobedience. If the events of Genesis did not happen as God said they did, then Christ's promises in the New Testament are meaningless, His cross is powerless, and His salvation and grace do not exist. Yet even in its corrupted state, the creation bears a residue of the "very good" state it once was, as well as the ingenious design in which our universe still functions. We observe this in all fields of scientific inquiry, from the inner workings of a plant cell to the structure and composition of galaxies in deep space.

The Foundation for the Sanctity of Human Life

The Bible teaches that human beings are qualitatively different from other organisms. We are made in the image of God and enjoy special rights and responsibilities that animals and plants do not. This is why it is fundamentally immoral to murder a human being, but it's okay to take advantage of God's permission to eat an animal (Genesis 9:3-4). Whether we admit it or not, we all recognize that human beings are not just another organism of the planet. We are set apart from animals and plants by the Creator Himself, having been made in His image.

The Foundation for Marriage

The Bible teaches that marriage is a holy union between one man and one woman for life. Several passages in Scripture address the topic of marriage, which God instituted on the sixth day of creation when He made Eve from Adam's side. Genesis 2:24 says that this historical event is the reason why we have marriage today: "Therefore a man shall leave his father and mother and be joined to his wife, and they shall become one flesh." God provided the prototype marriage at the creation, and Jesus affirmed this in Matthew 19:4-6.

The Foundation for Rest and Worship

Most cultures on Earth have a seven-day week, but where does this idea come from? And why rest one day in seven, as opposed to ten or five? Genesis 1:1–2:2 indicates that God created in six days and then rested one day. Exodus 20:11 specifically explains that the creation week is the basis for our work week, and that the day of rest is set aside to enjoy and worship our Creator.

The Curse

God cursed Earth after the Fall of Adam and Eve. We can see that something changed at the Curse. It is mankind, not God, who is to blame for sin and death in this world. Scripture clearly states that God's original creation was "very good." After the Curse, it deteriorated, and certain parts of the creation have changed to become "imperfect." This is the origin of predatory and parasitic behaviors in certain organisms.

Cursed is the ground for your sake; In toil you shall eat of it All the days of your life. Both thorns and thistles it shall bring forth for you, And you shall eat the herb of the field. In the sweat of your face you shall eat bread Till you return to the ground, For out of it you were taken; For dust you are, And to dust you shall return. (Genesis 3:17-19)

BACTERIA AND VIRUSES

Today there are increasing discoveries indicating that "bad" (pathogenic) bacteria, parasites, and viruses may have had a more neutral or even beneficial function prior to the Fall. For example, *Escherichia coli* (*E. coli*) bacteria can either be good or bad depending on the subspecies and where it is found in the body. In the colon, the bacteria make important B vitamins and vitamin K. If the colon is ruptured, however, *E. coli* escaping into the body cavity can have fatal consequences. Also, humans and animals have been created with poisons called caspases built into cells. Caspases are part of the critical process of programmed cell death (apoptosis) and recycling.

MORE BENEFICIAL BACTERIA

Under different conditions, disease-causing bacteria in nature have had beneficial applications. The pathogenic bacteria called *Vibrio cholerae* can cause the small intestine infection cholera in people. The bacteria secrete a deadly toxin similar to one produced by *V. fischeri*, a curious light-emitting symbiotic bacterium found in the Hawaiian bobtail squid. The squid uses the luminescent properties of the bacteria to evade predators in the clear water where it feeds. Light from the bacteria, aided by a reflector, is radiated downward in a way that counters the moonlight, putting the squid in a "stealth mode." When the bacteria get hungry, they secrete the cholera-like toxin that doesn't sicken the squid, but informs it that they need food, which the squid then provides.

SHARP TEETH AND CLAWS

At first glance, animals with sharp teeth and claws appear to be equipped only to eat other animals. However, it seems that sharp teeth and claws are perfectly suited for breaking through the tough skins of some fruits. Certain types of bats consume insects, other small animals, and blood. However, they can also eat flower nectar and fruit. Fruit bats consume only fruit, even though they have sharp teeth and claws like other bats. This shows the accuracy of God's Word that every created being was originally vegetarian: "'Also, to every beast of the earth, to every bird of the air, and to everything that creeps on the earth, in which there is life, I have given every green herb for food'; and it was so" (Genesis 1:30).

THE PANDA'S DIGESTIVE TRACT

Carnivores have short digestive tracts, but herbivores have long digestive tracts so that they can break down the large amounts of fiber in their foods. Panda bears, like other bears, have short digestive tracts and yet live on primarily a vegetarian diet.

PARASITISM

A parasite is a type of animal (or plant) that lives together in close, non-mutual association with a usually larger organism called the host. The word "parasite" comes from a Greek word meaning a person who eats at another's table. For example, malaria parasites are single-cell organisms that live in the liver and red blood cells of a victim after the person is bitten by an infected mosquito. The tiny parasites eat the red pigment in the blood cells, reproduce, and are shielded from the person's immune system.

Before the Fall, parasites were evidently complete, non-parasitic organisms. Many parasites today are little more than protoplasmic bags of reproductive structures with an attachment (hooks or suckers) on one end. They may have lost much of their genetic information as a result of the Curse. As fallen creatures, we see parasites as a reminder of how today's world is still "good-yet-groaning" as we await the ultimate redemption of creation promised in Romans 8:20-22.

PREDATOR/PREY RELATIONSHIPS

Since there was no death before Adam and Eve sinned, there were no predator/prey relationships in God's original perfect creation. However, certain animal kinds that include predators also have varieties that can survive on mostly vegetarian diets, such as bears and bats. Domesticated animals such as dogs and cats can live on food mostly made of corn. The fact that the same types of animals can display both carnivore and herbivore behavior reflects a once "very good" creation that is now fallen.

Origin of People Groups and Languages

All people descended recently from a single family. We understand that from Scripture and see it supported by the findings of scientific inquiry.

For instance, the book of Genesis states that "Adam called his wife's name Eve, because she was the mother of all living" (Genesis 3:20). Mitochondria inside cells are inherited solely through the egg from the mother, allowing the identification of descendants from any female lineage. Variations in mitochondrial DNA between people have conclusively shown that all people have descended from one female, just as it is stated in Scripture. The instability of the mitochondrial genome and computer simulations modeling mutation load in humans indicate that the human mitochondrial genome is not that old, which fits within a biblical timeframe.

> "He has made from one blood every nation of men to dwell on all the face of the earth." (Acts 17:26)

Y chromosomes are passed on to sons from their fathers. Just as mitochondrial DNA shows that every human descended from one female, Y chromosome analysis suggests that all men have descended from one man. Blood type studies, genetic mutation load, and various other studies also support the idea that humans have been around (complete and not evolved) for about the same amount of time as Scripture records.

RACE

Since the dispersion at Babel, we have seen only variation within the created kind of people. That means there are no separate races (Acts 17:26). We are all people that vary in function and form. We also don't have different colors. Melanin is the pigment that gives our skin its color. All humans have melanin (except for people with the condition known as albinism—the absence of melanin), but some people have more melanin than others. In short, we're technically all the same color, but we just have different shades of that color.

MIGRATION

After the Flood, God instructed Noah and the seven members of his family who survived aboard the Ark to "be fruitful, and multiply, and replenish the earth" (Genesis 9:1, KJV). Instead, their descendants assembled at Babel under the leadership of a defiant man named Nimrod. The disobedient populace united and revolted against God by building a tower. But God separated their single language into many, preventing their ability to communicate, as well as cooperate to continue their rebellion. This confusion caused them to disperse throughout the earth (Genesis 11:6-8), as He had commanded earlier, and into the people groups that we know today.

GENETIC ENTROPY

The second law of thermodynamics, also known as the law of entropy, states that the entropy of an isolated system that is not in equilibrium, such as the universe, will tend to increase over time. Humans are not exempt from this (due to the Curse), so our genetic information is increasingly moving from a state of order to a state of disorder (entropy). We observe this especially in the form of genetic mutations. While God created our systems to be quite robust, the amount of genetic mutations is increasing from generation to generation. Based on the results of genetic studies, the human race is about as old as the Bible says. If we were much older, we would be extinct just from the sheer amount of genetic mutations.

LANGUAGE

In the Table of Nations recorded in Genesis 10, we see that 70 family groups (nations) migrated from Babel to parts all around the world. Linguistic studies have shown that the number of separate language groups is basically the same as the 70 listed in Scripture.

Design in Creation

Our world is generally wild and untamed, and yet everything in nature follows a specific order. Complicated systems or structures do not happen spontaneously, and we never observe complexity occurring by accident or without an intelligent cause to direct the order. No amount of power or energy is enough on its own to bring complexity out of chaos, which means the order we observe must be designed by God. There are not enough books in the history of the world that could record all the design and order aspects of creation, but just a glimpse at a few examples can demonstrate God's ingenuity, power, and dedication.

TIMES AND SEASONS

God promised in Genesis 8:22, "While the earth remains, Seedtime and harvest, Cold and heat, Winter and summer, And day and night Shall not cease." The climate and length of daylight may be different in different parts of the world, but our planet follows set patterns—and patterns never mean a random or disorderly source.

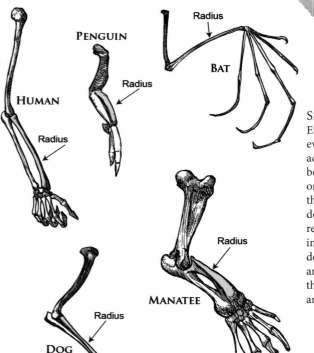

SIMILAR DESIGN IN SIMILAR BODY PARTS

Evolutionists like to say that similarities in living things mean that they evolved from a common ancestor or ancestors that lived eons ago. But what we actually see in similar features is *similar design*. For instance, humans have a radius bone in the forearm, the same place where penguins, dogs, and other animals have one. Along with similarly placed joints, digits (e.g., fingers), and other structures, the radius is part of a good design. Human engineers know that re-using a good design (e.g., four wheels in most vehicles) is efficient, rather than having to redesign something each time. So, it makes sense that God used a good design in more than one living thing. Mice and frogs have radii bones too, but they are developed from different embryonic tissue. If they had evolved from the same ancestor, then those bones would have developed from the same tissue. The fact that they did not develop from the same tissue means that they were designed, and design always means that a designer made them.

DESIGN IN THE DETAILS

Perhaps nothing in the world is as versatile and useful a tool as the human hand. Its details constantly display real design. For example, fingerbone lengths follow the proportions of the Fibonacci number sequence—the sum of the smallest two segments of a finger equals the length of the third, and the sum of the second and third equals the length of the fourth bone (the one backing the palm). Your hand is a mobile golden spiral, perfectly balancing strength and dexterity. Hand muscles actually reside in the forearm, giving the palm space to hold an object or another person's hand. Extended fingers squeezed against one another show the offset knuckles meshing. If knuckles lined up, they'd rub uncomfortably and space fingers too far apart. Unlike ape hands, the lengths and strengths of human finger and thumb bones are just right for manipulating objects. Tightly clenched fingers don't displace one another. Their balanced strengths help the hand keep a steady grip. And how do people type so fast? The brain plans finger movements three actions ahead of time. Hands are full of the kinds of details that we know always originate from an intelligent and purposeful source.

DID YOU KNOW?

When you eat, you're essentially eating energy from the sun. Plants need sunlight to grow, and humans and animals eat plants to live. Even when we eat animals (usually herbivores), we're indirectly consuming the energy from the sun that was transferred through the plants they ate.

PERFECT PROVISION

Energy is required for things to happen, but not all forms of energy are useful for every purpose. For instance, burning wood is a source of energy, but humans can't eat fire and keep living. Likewise, burning an apple won't do you much good if you want to heat your home. In Genesis 1:29, God said to Adam, "I have given you every herb that yields seed which is on the face of all the earth, and every tree whose fruit yields seed; to you it shall be for food." He made food specifically for humans and animals to consume. Not only that, He didn't make the earth yield just one type of food, but a variety. By designing the earth to provide food for humans, God made it possible for humans—even in our current corrupted state—to fulfill His blessing and command to "fill the earth and subdue [or take care of] it" (Genesis 1:28).

Numbers in Nature

The field of mathematics is an interesting one, and it has taken intelligent humans to discover and understand how numbers work. One was a man named Leonardo of Pisa, also known as Fibonacci. In 1202, he published a book called *Liber Abaci* in which he introduced the sequence named after him to Western European mathematics. Before him, Indian mathematics described the same sequence. Evolution has no explanation for the development of mathematical laws, but they are easily accounted for in Scripture by an intelligent Creator.

From Fibonacci's *Liber Abaci* showing the Fibonacci sequence in the box to the right.

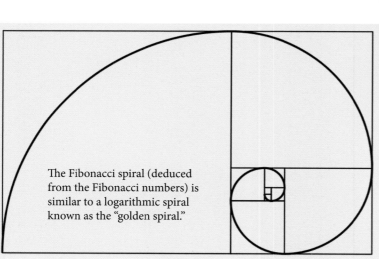

The Fibonacci spiral (deduced from the Fibonacci numbers) is similar to a logarithmic spiral known as the "golden spiral."

$$F_n - F_{n-1} + F_{n-2}$$

with seed values

$$F_0 = 0, \ F_1 = 1$$

Fibonacci Formula

0, 1, 1, 2, 3, 5, 8, 13, 21, 34, 55, 89, 144 . . .

FIBONACCI SEQUENCE
The first two numbers in the Fibonacci sequence are 0 and 1. Each number after is the sum of the previous two numbers.

Snowflakes are another example of mathematics in nature. The complex and beautiful patterns form when supercooled cloud droplets combine and form a crystal lattice. Snowflakes have a self-repeating "fractal" quality, much like the graphs of certain mathematical algorithms. Why is this so? The laws of nature responsible for snowflake formation are mathematical because they stem from the mind of God. But in a chance universe why would nature obey math?

Fibonacci sequences can appear in nature, such as in the branch patterns of trees, the flowering of an artichoke, leaf arrangement on a stem, and the structure of a pine cone. Just as design in nature points to a designer, this orderly mathematical sequence points to a master mathematician.

Logarithmic spirals are a type of spiral curve that often appears in nature. The French philosopher and mathematician René Descartes (1596-1650) first described the logarithmic spiral, and the Swiss mathematician Jacob Bernoulli (1655-1705) expounded on it. Nautilus shells, romanesco broccoli, and the Whirlpool Galaxy are examples that have the shape of a logarithmic spiral.

Humans Are Unique

Scripture clearly states that humans are unlike any other part of God's creation. Although our genetics and appearance are different from animals, there are less apparent—but more important—reasons than just our genome that determine the nature of humans. Genesis reveals that God created us in His image, a quality that separates us from the rest of creation. This explains why our behavior is far more complex than any other living thing on the planet. We are able to imagine and create objects never seen before (art, buildings, etc.), show compassion for strangers, and ponder our role and fate in creation.

Humans also differ from the other creatures in our relationship to God. We were created to serve Him, and we are His most treasured creation. God treasures us so much that He died to reconcile us to Himself. It is this value that God places on humans that truly separates us from the rest of creation. Since God created, saved, and continually sustains us, why wouldn't we want to offer all our worship and gratitude to Him?

Just like the beautiful variety of flower colors around the world, eye color serves no evolutionary purpose—neither makes survival either better or more difficult. Instead, flower and eye color show God's appreciation of beauty and creative tastes.

Then God said, "Let Us make man in Our image, according to Our likeness; let them have dominion over the fish of the sea, over the birds of the air, and over the cattle, over all the earth and over every creeping thing that creeps on the earth." So God created man in His own image; in the image of God He created him; male and female He created them. Then God blessed them, and God said to them, "Be fruitful and multiply; fill the earth and subdue it; have dominion over the fish of the sea, over the birds of the air, and over every living thing that moves on the earth." (Genesis 1:26-28)

LITTLE "CREATORS"
We observe animals building structures such as homes and dams, similar to how humans build things. However, animals do so by reacting to the instincts God built into them. Humans, on the other hand, are the only creatures that can make things out of their imaginations. We also are the only creatures that produce work purely for intellectual and aesthetic purposes. This book in your hand is an example of that.

HIS IMAGE

Human bodies are made of the same "earth" material as the animals (Genesis 2:7, 19) and the planet itself (Genesis 1:10). Furthermore, we share the created "soul" (Hebrew *nephesh*) and "spirit" (Hebrew *ruach*, same as "breath") with the animals. However, we alone bear the created "image of God" (Genesis 1:27). That is why when Christ came, He came as a human.

MADE FOR WORSHIP

Humans are the only creatures that worship something. The vast majority of humans identify with some sort of religion, showing our innate longing to be connected to our Creator and heavenly Father. Genesis 3:8 states that God was "walking in the garden [of which He put Adam and Eve in charge] in the cool of the day," showing that He regularly "hung out" with His created humans. Adam and Eve's rebellion broke that connection with God, and the human struggles with idolatry throughout history were poor attempts to fill our need to reconnect with our Creator. Thankfully, God did what we could not do for ourselves and implemented His redemption plan by coming, dying, and rising again in the form of Jesus Christ to re-establish that connection. Does that not make Him worth our worship?

STEWARDS OF GOD'S CREATION

When God created the first humans (Adam and Eve), He blessed and commissioned them to care for the earth He created. God never ordered them (and by extension us) to abuse His creation, especially for greedy purposes. Responsible stewardship consists of 1) responsible environmental management, including consideration for the preservation of the ecosystem and provision for basic human needs; 2) not engaging in reproductive technologies that intentionally destroy human life or create human life for experimentation; and 3) the application of biotechnology to provide relief from human suffering, while not encouraging human genetic or cybernetic enhancement that provides "superhuman" qualities.

Index

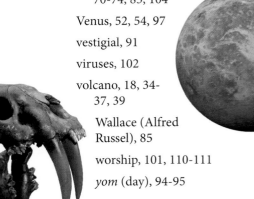

ICR Contributors

Henry M. Morris III, D. Min.
CHIEF EXECUTIVE OFFICER

Dr. Henry Morris III holds four earned degrees, including a D.Min. from Luther Rice Seminary and the Presidents and Key Executives MBA from Pepperdine University. A former college professor, administrator, business executive, and senior pastor, he is the eldest son of the Institute for Creation Research's founder. Dr. Morris has served for many years in conference and writing ministry.

John D. Morris, Ph.D.
PRESIDENT EMERITUS

Dr. John Morris, perhaps best known for leading expeditions to Mt. Ararat in search of Noah's Ark, received his doctorate in geological engineering at the University of Oklahoma in 1980. He served on the University of Oklahoma faculty before joining the Institute for Creation Research in 1984. Dr. Morris held the position of professor of geology and was appointed president in 1996. He continues to serve ICR as President Emeritus.

James J. S. Johnson, J.D., Th.D.
CHIEF ACADEMIC OFFICER

Dr. James Johnson received his J.D. in 1984 from the University of North Carolina, which included studies at Duke University Law School, and in 1996 obtained his Th.D. His educational background includes earned degrees in religion and the natural sciences. For his scholarship in biblical languages and their cognates, Dr. Johnson was awarded the American Bible Society Award in 1982. He currently serves as Chief Academic Officer of ICR's School of Biblical Apologetics.

Randy Guliuzza, P.E., M.D.
NATIONAL REPRESENTATIVE

Dr. Randy Guliuzza has a B.S. in engineering from the South Dakota School of Mines and Technology, a B.A. in theology from Moody Bible Institute, an M.D. from the University of Minnesota, and a Master's in Public Health from Harvard University. Dr. Guliuzza served nine years in the Navy Civil Engineer Corps and is a registered professional engineer. In 2008, he retired as Lt. Col. from the U.S. Air Force, where he served as Flight Surgeon and Chief of Aerospace Medicine.

Jeffrey Tomkins, Ph.D.
DIRECTOR OF LIFE SCIENCES

Dr. Jeffrey Tomkins earned a master's degree in plant science in 1990 from the University of Idaho, where he performed research in plant hormones. He received his Ph.D. in genetics from Clemson University in 1996. While at Clemson, he worked as a research technician in a plant breeding/genetics program, with a research focus in the area of quantitative and physiological genetics in soybean.

Leo (Jake) Hebert III, Ph.D.
Research Associate

Dr. Jake Hebert earned a master's degree in physics in 1999 from Texas A&M University, where he studied optics and was a Dean's Graduate Fellow 1995-1996. He received his Ph.D. in 2011 from the University of Texas at Dallas, where his research involved a study of the possible connection between fair-weather atmospheric electricity and climate.

Frank Sherwin, M.A.
Research Associate, Senior Lecturer, and Science Writer

Frank Sherwin received his bachelor's degree in biology from Western State College, Gunnison, Colorado, in 1978. He attended graduate school at the University of Northern Colorado, where he studied under the late Gerald D. Schmidt, one of the foremost parasitologists in America. During his time in graduate school, Mr. Sherwin discovered a new species of parasite, the study of which was published in a peer-reviewed secular journal. In 1985, Mr. Sherwin obtained a masters degree in zoology.

Brian Thomas, M.S.
Science Writer

Brian Thomas received his bachelor's degree in biology from Stephen F. Austin State University, Nacogdoches, Texas, in 1993. After beginning graduate studies at the Institute for Creation Research Graduate School, he returned to Stephen F. Austin, where he earned a master's degree in biotechnology in 1999. He taught biology and chemistry at high school and undergraduate levels.

Jason Lisle, Ph.D.

Dr. Jason Lisle graduated summa cum laude from Ohio Wesleyan University, where he double-majored in physics and astronomy and minored in mathematics. He earned a master's degree and a Ph.D. in astrophysics at the University of Colorado. Dr. Lisle specialized in solar astrophysics and has made a number of scientific discoveries regarding the solar photosphere and has contributed to the field of general relativity.

Nathaniel Jeanson, Ph.D.

Dr. Nathaniel Jeanson received his Ph.D. in cell and developmental biology from Harvard Medical School in 2009. While at Harvard, he assisted in adult stem cell research, specifically on the role of Vitamin D in regulating blood stem cells. Dr. Jeanson has a B.S. in Molecular Biology and Bioinformatics from the University of Wisconsin-Parkside.

Contributors

Susan Windsor, Graphic Designer at ICR, provided some original illustrations, graphic design expertise, and her unique artistic style in the creation of this book.

Jayme Durant, Director of Communications and Executive Editor at ICR, developed the Guide to… series concept as well as the content throughout this book.

Susan Windsor   Jayme Durant

Image Credits

t-top; m-middle; b-bottom; c-center; l-left; r-right

Bigstock Photo: 10, 11, 12, 13t, 14t,bl,mr,br, 15tr, 15mc, mb, mr, 18, 19t, l, 20b, 21m, 22b, 23b, 25tl, tr, b, 26-27, 29tl, bl, br, 30t, 31tl, tm, lc, lb, rb, 34bl, br, 35br, 38tr, ml, 39br, 40r, 41br, 42tr, m, 43tr, b, 44, 48tr, ml, bl, 49m, tr, 50tr, 55t, 60tr, bl, 61bl, br, 62, 64tr, 65br, 66, 67, 68bl, br, 69ml, 70, 71bl, bm, br, 72bm, br, 73, 76l, 77, 78, 79tl, m, b, 80tr, 81tl, bl, 82-83 (silhouette), 84r, 86t, 87tr, 88bl, 89bm, br, 90bl, tr, 91bl, br, tr, 93tl, bl, 95 (background), 96tr, 97m, tr, 98-99, 100, 101, 102, 103tr, m, mr, br, bl, bm, 104, 105t, 106tr, tl, bm, br, 107, 109tl, mr, 110tr, bl, 111

Fotolia: 14bc, 15mt, mr, 21b, 38b, 71ml, 76br, 97br, 103tl

Jens L. Franzen, Philip D. Gingerich, Jörg Habersetzer1, Jørn H. Hurum, Wighart von Koenigswald, B. Holly Smith (Wikipedia): 89

Google Earth: 20t

ICR: 19br, 21t, 24, 28-29m, tr, 30ml, 31mr, 33mr, 42b, 43tl, 45tl, mr, 74, 75, 87br, 106bl

iStock Photo: 13b, 43m, 49br, 64br, 65tr, ml, 68bc, 69tr, rm, 71tl, tr, mr, 72l, 80bl, 88tr, tm, bm, br, mrc, 109bl, 110mr

John Morris: 36, 37l

NASA: 15tl, ml, bl, 16-17, 46-47, 50m, b, 51, 52, 53r, ml, 54, 56, 57, 58, 59, 61tl, 82-83 (background), 96bl,

National Science Foundation: 86b

Pacific Northwest National Laboratory: 45b

Public Domain: 24b, 32m, b, 38mc, 39mr, 40t, l, 41tr, l, 48r, 49bl, 53tl, 60br, 64mr, 79tr, 84l, 85, 87bl, 89l, 92, 93br, 95mr, 105b, 108

Public Library of Science (PLoS): 32-33t

Daryl Robbins: 81mr

Brian Thomas: 25mr

U.S. Geological Survey: 35tr, 37r, 39tl

The Children's Museum of Indianapolis: 80br

Susan Windsor: 22t, 23tl, tr, 30b, 34t, 35bl, 55b, 68tr, 69b, 91tm, 93tr, 94tr

About the Institute for Creation Research

After almost five decades of ministry, the Institute for Creation Research remains a leader in scientific research within the context of biblical creation. Founded by Dr. Henry Morris in 1970, ICR exists to conduct scientific research within the realms of origins and Earth history and then to educate the public both formally and informally through graduate and professional training programs, through conferences and seminars around the country, and through books, magazines, and media presentations. ICR was established for three main purposes:

Dr. Henry Morris

Research. ICR conducts laboratory, field, theoretical, and library research on projects that seek to understand the science of origins and Earth history. ICR scientists have conducted multi-year research projects at key locations such as Grand Canyon, Mount St. Helens, Yosemite Valley, Santa Cruz River Valley in Argentina, and on vital issues like Radioisotopes and the Age of the Earth (RATE), Flood-Activated Sedimentation and Tectonics (FAST), the human genome, and other topics related to geology, genetics, astro/geophysics, paleoclimatology, and much more.

Education. ICR offers formal courses of instruction and conducts seminars and workshops, as well as other means of instruction. With over 30 years of experience in graduate education, first through our California-based science education program (1981-2010), and now through the degree programs at the School of Biblical Apologetics, ICR trains men and women to do real-world apologetics with a foundation of biblical authority and creation science. ICR also offers a one-year, non-degree training program for professionals called the Creationist Worldview. Additionally, ICR scientists and staff speak to over 200 groups each year through seminars and conferences.

Communication. ICR produces books, videos, periodicals, and other media for communicating the evidence and information related to its research and education. ICR's central publication is *Acts & Facts*, a free full-color monthly magazine with a readership of over 250,000, providing articles relevant to science, apologetics, education, and worldview issues. ICR also publishes the daily devotional *Days of Praise* with over 500,000 readers worldwide. Our website at ICR.org features regular and relevant creation science updates. The three radio programs produced by ICR can be heard on outlets around the world, and we make our materials available through multiple social media outlets.

Founded in southern California but now headquartered in Dallas, Texas, the Institute for Creation Research continues to expand its work and influence in each of these areas of ministry, endeavoring to encourage Christians with the wonders of God's creation.

P. O. Box 59029
Dallas, Texas 75229
ICR.org

800.337.0375 (main) | 800.628.7640 (customer service)